QUILTING WITH FONS & PORTER

ISBN: 0-9676310-1-7
Printed in the United States of America
First Printing 2000
Published by Fons & Porter, L.C.
P.O. Box 171
Winterset, IA 50273
www.fonsandporter.com

© 2000 by Marianne Fons & Liz Porter

All rights reserved. No part of this book may be reproduced in any form or by an means without the prior written permission of the publisher, excepting brief quotations in connection with reviews written specifically for inclusion in magazines or newspapers.

TABLE OF CONTENTS

(Larger Titles Denote Projects in Book.)

ABOUT THIS BOOK

This book is a companion to our television series "Quilting with Fons & Porter," but you can easily make these projects whether you've seen us on TV or not! We've included full instructions for each quilt, along with many helpful tips to make your quilting easy and fun.

When using the book, keep in mind that all patchwork seams are ¼". Seam allowances are included in the cutting sizes for patchwork. Cut strips crosswise unless directed otherwise. Border dimensions are given exact size—you may wish to add an extra inch or so when cutting (for "accident insurance"). Trim to exact size before adding borders to your quilt.

Appliqué patterns are printed finished size. For hand appliqué, add ³⁄₁₆" when cutting out shapes. For fusible methods, cut appliqué pieces finished size.

For basic quilt making instructions, see our *Quilter's Complete Guide*, a 256-page text that gives techniques and guidelines for all aspects of quilting. To order a copy, call 1-888-985-1020. Price is $29.95 hardcover or $19.95 softcover, plus shipping and handling.

DIAGONAL SEAMS PATCHWORK

Several of the projects in this book call for the "diagonal seams" technique. This method enables you to create various types of patchwork units (including many tricky-to-cut units) by using easy-to-cut squares and rectangles. Basically, the diagonal seams method involves placing a square atop some other shape and sewing from one corner to the opposite diagonal corner.

SETTING UP YOUR SEWING MACHINE

1. Raise presser foot and lower needle to a fully "down" position. Place a ruler on the throat plate so that ruler edge is against needle. Lower presser foot to hold ruler in place. Be sure lines on ruler are square and parallel to lines on throat plate.
2. Place a 2½"-long strip of masking tape on throat plate, along straight edge of ruler so edge of tape creates a line straight out from needle. (Instead of tape, we sometimes use a "sticky note" that is easily removed when we aren't sewing diagonal seams.)
3. Lift presser foot and remove ruler. Raise needle.
4. When stitching diagonal seams units, guide bottom corner of square (side closest to you as you sew) along edge of tape guide to keep stitching straight.

SEWING DIAGONAL SEAMS

Each project includes instructions on sizes to cut pieces for diagonal seams and diagrams for how to sew the diagonal seams. For example, to make a Goose Chase unit, you might be asked to cut 2 (2½") light squares and 1 (2½" x 4½") dark rectangle.

1. Place 1 (2½") square atop 1 end of the 2½" x 4½" rectangle. Stitch diagonally as shown in *Diagram 1*.
2. Open out the square, forming a triangle, and check to see that edges of square are aligned with edges of rectangle.
3. Trim excess square and rectangle beyond diagonal stitching line, leaving approximately ¼" for seam allowance as shown in *Diagram 2*. Open out triangle as shown in *Diagram 3*.
4. In a similar manner, add a square to the other side of the rectangle as shown in *Diagram 4*. Open out square, trim, and press to make Goose Chase unit as shown in *Diagram 5*.

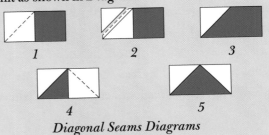

Diagonal Seams Diagrams

COLORBOX ABCS QUILT

Liz chose brightly colored juvenile fabrics for the backgrounds of her letter blocks. To make the letters stand out against these busy background fabrics, she used coordinating solid colors for the letters.

Designed and pieced by
Liz Porter
Machine quilted by
Lynn Witzenburg

Finished size	60" x 71½"
Blocks	26 (9") Letter blocks and
	4 (9") Pinwheel blocks

MATERIALS

❏ 1 yard of turquoise solid fabric for Pinwheel blocks, letters, sashing squares, and binding

❏ 1¾ yards of multi-color stripe fabric for sashing strips

❏ ½ yard of red print for Pinwheel blocks and background of 2 letter blocks

❏ ½ yard of yellow print for Pinwheel blocks and background of 2 letter blocks

❏ Fat quarter* each of 1 red, 1 orange, 1 hot pink, 1 yellow, 1 turquoise, 2 green, 2 purple, and 2 blue juvenile novelty prints for backgrounds of letter blocks

❏ Fat quarter* each of yellow, green, yellow-green, red, orange, dark purple, medium purple, hot pink, and royal blue solid fabrics for letters

❏ 3¾ yards of fabric for quilt back

❏ Twin-size quilt batting

*Fat quarter = 18" x 22"

CUTTING

Measurements include ¼" seam allowances. Cut strips across fabric width. Cut pieces for letter blocks by referring to Graphed Letters on page 10. Each square on graph will equal 1" to make letters that finish 5" tall before framing. Letters are assembled by using either diagonal seams or foundation piecing. Refer to Patchwork Alphabets on pages 6-9.

From turquoise solid fabric, cut:
- 7 (2¼"-wide) strips for binding.
- 1 (5¾"-wide) strip. From this, cut 4 (5¾") squares. Cut each square in quarters diagonally to make a total of 16 quarter-square A triangles for Pinwheel blocks.

From multi-color stripe, cut:
- 18 (3"-wide) strips. From these, cut 71 (3" x 9½") sashing rectangles.

From ½ yard of red print fabric, cut:
- 1 (5⅜"-wide) strip. From this, cut 8 (5⅜") squares. Cut each square in half diagonally to make a total of 16 half-square B triangles for Pinwheel blocks.

From ½ yard of yellow print fabric, cut:
- 1 (5¾"-wide) strip. From this, cut 4 (5¾") squares. Cut each square in quarters diagonally to make a total of 16 quarter-square A triangles for Pinwheel blocks.

From assorted solid color fat quarters, cut:
- 42 (3") sashing squares.

PINWHEEL BLOCK ASSEMBLY

1. Referring to *Block Assembly Diagram*, join yellow A triangle to turquoise A triangle to form pieced triangle unit. Join pieced triangle unit to red B triangle to form A/B square unit. Repeat to make 4 A/B square units.
2. Join A/B units into 2 rows; join rows. Repeat to make 4 Pinwheel blocks as shown in *Block Diagram*.

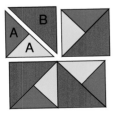
Block Assembly Diagram

Block Diagram

LETTER BLOCK ASSEMBLY

1. Referring to Patchwork Alphabets on pages 6-9, assemble letters using either diagonal seams, foundation piecing, or a combination of techniques.
2. From block background fabrics, cut strips as needed to make blocks that finish 9" square. Sew strips to block sides. Repeat to add strips to top and bottom edges of blocks.

QUILT ASSEMBLY

1. Referring to photograph, lay out letter blocks in alphabetical order and Pinwheel blocks at quilt corners, making 6 horizontal rows with 5 blocks in each row. Lay out sashing rectangles and sashing squares.
2. Make block rows by joining 5 blocks and 6 sashing strips. Make 6 block rows.
3. Make sashing rows by joining 6 assorted color sashing squares and 5 sashing strips. Make 7 sashing rows.
4. Join block rows and sashing rows, alternating types.

FINISHING

1. Mark quilting designs as desired.
2. Divide backing fabric into 2 (1⅞-yard) panels. Split 1 panel in half lengthwise. Join half panels to sides of full panel. Press seam allowances away from center panel. Seams on quilt back will run parallel to top edge of quilt.
3. Layer quilt back, batting, and quilt top; baste.
4. Quilt as desired. Quilt shown was machine quilted with interwoven wavy lines in block backgrounds, a cable in sashing strips, and a star variation in sashing squares.

PATCHWORK ALPHABETS

Pieced lettering on antique quilts has always intrigued us. When we decided to try patchwork wording our-selves, we designed a special alphabet that would make the piecing as easy as possible. Most of the letters in our alphabet are super simple—you can quick-cut the pieces with your rotary cutter and use the "diagonal seams" method to create the serifs (serifs are the parts of the letters that stick out at the ends of the letter strokes) and round off parts of letters. A few of our let-ters (K, M, N, W, X, and Z) and some of the numbers (2 and 7) require simple foundation piecing. We've included full-size foundation patterns for those letters and numbers in the sizes needed for Liz's Colorbox ABCs quilt (5"-tall letters) and for Marianne's Alphabet Mini (2½"-tall letters).

The graphed alphabet is on page 10, and the graphed numbers are on page 9. To use the graphs, decide what scale you want for your letters. For Liz's Colorbox ABCs quilt, each square on the graph equals 1". For Marianne's Alphabet Mini, each square equals ½". For each letter, count the number of squares in the length and width of each element of the letter; then, add ½" each way to the total for seam allowances. Where you see triangle serifs on letters, or triangle areas in the background that help form the letter, cut a square or rectangle and use diagonal seams to piece that part of the letter. (See Diagonal Seams Patchwork on page 3 if you are not familiar with this piecing method.)

MAKING LETTER A

Get started making pieced letters by stitching a sample letter A. You'll need scraps of two fabrics, one light and one dark. For the sample letter, each square equals 1", like Liz's quilt. The letter is five squares tall, and the block divides into five vertical rows.

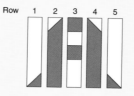

Block Assembly Diagram

Block Diagram

CUTTING

From light fabric, cut:
- 2 (1½" x 5½") rectangles for Rows 1 and 5
- 1 (1½" x 2½") rectangle for Row 3
- 3 (1½") squares for Rows 2, 3, and 4

From dark fabric, cut:
- 4 (1½") squares for Rows 1, 3, and 5
- 2 (1½" x 5½") rectangles for Rows 2 and 4

PIECING

1. To make Row 1, place dark square atop end of light (1½" x 5½") rectangle with right sides facing as shown in *Row A-1 Diagrams*.

2. Stitch diagonally. Open out dark square to form tri-angle, comparing unit to graphed illustration to make sure angle is correct. Trim ¼" from stitching.

3. Repeat to make Row 5, changing angle of stitching as shown in *Row A-5 Diagrams*.

Row A-1 Diagrams

Row A-5 Diagrams

4. To make Row 2, place light square atop end of dark (1½" x 5½") rectangle with right sides facing as shown in *Row A-2 Diagrams*. Stitch diagonally, open out square to form triangle, and trim.

5. Make Row 4 in a similar manner to Row 2, changing angle of diagonal stitching as shown in *Row A-4 Diagrams*.

Row A-2 Diagrams　　　*Row A-4 Diagrams*

6. To make Row 3, join squares and rectangles as shown in *Row A-3 Diagrams*.

7. Join rows to complete letter A.

Row A-3 Diagrams

PIECING OTHER BASIC LETTERS AND NUMBERS

For each letter or number you make, look at the graph and analyze the elements of the letter. For another example, take a look at the diagrams for the letter P, and study the vertical rows that make up the letter.

Block Assembly Diagram　　*Block Diagram*

If you are working with 1 square = 1", for Row 1 you'll use diagonal seams to add 2 (1½") dark squares to 1 (1½" x 5½") light rectangle. Row 2 is a simple 1½" x 5½" dark rectangle. Row 3 looks a little tricky at first, but it is simple too. The bottom half of the row is a 2½" light square. The top half of the row is made of two sections. For the left section, join 2 (1½") dark squares and 1 (1½") light square. For the right section, use diagonal seams to add 2 (1½") light squares to 1 (1½" x 3½") dark rectangle.

Look over the entire alphabet and the numbers and think through how you would construct each letter. Patchwork letters are fun to make!

A FEW TRICKY LETTERS

You might need a helping hand as you analyze and construct a few of the letters in our alphabet. Letters B, G, R, and S involve diagonal seams piecing that is a little more challenging than the other letters. Use the diagrams to help you cut and sew the pieces. To give you a bit more help, we've written detailed instructions for the tricky parts of these letters. The sizes given are for a 1" finished grid to make 5"-tall letters. Sizes in parenthesis are for a ½" finished grid to make 2½"-tall letters.

LETTER B

The far right row (Row 4) of the letter B is a bit tricky to piece. It is made in two halves.

Block Assembly Diagram　　*Block Diagram*

To make the top half, cut a 1½" (1") light square, a 1" (½") light square, and a 1½" x 3½" (1" x 2") dark rectangle. Join pieces with diagonal seams as shown in *Top Half of Row 4 Assembly Diagrams*. Cut identical pieces and make the bottom half of the row in a similar manner.

Top Half of Row 4 Assembly Diagrams

LETTER G

For the third section of Row 2 of the letter G, cut a 1½" x 2½" (1" x 1½") light rectangle. Cut matching pieces from dark fabric. Join pieces with diagonal seams as shown in *Section of Row 2 Assembly Diagrams.*

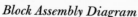

Block Assembly Diagram   *Block Diagram*

Section of Row 2 Assembly Diagrams

LETTER S

To make the left row (Row 1), cut two 1½"(1") squares and a 1½" x 2½"(1" x 1½") rectangle of light fabric. From dark fabric, cut a 1½" x 3½" (1" x 2") rectangle and a 1½" x 2½" (1" x 1½") rectangle. Join pieces as shown in *Row 1 Assembly Diagrams.* Cut identical pieces for the right row (Row 3) and join in a similar manner.

Block Assembly Diagram   *Block Diagram*

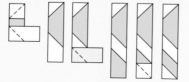

Row 1 Assembly Diagrams

LETTER R

To make the far right row (Row 4), cut a 1½" (1") square and a 1½" x 3½" (1" x 2") rectangle from light fabric. Cut a 1½" (1") square and a 1½" x 3½" (1" x 2") rectangle from dark fabric. Join pieces as shown in *Row 4 Assembly Diagrams.*

Block Assembly Diagram   *Block Diagram*

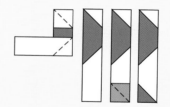

Row 4 Assembly Diagrams

FOUNDATION LETTERS AND NUMBERS

All but six of the graphed letters and two of the numbers are pieced as described above using the diagonal seams method. The letters K, M, N, W, X, and Z and numbers 2 and 7 have portions that are pieced on a paper foundation.

Foundation piecing is a method of patchwork that involves stitching through a paper pattern. It is ideal for small, intricate designs or designs with odd angles and sizes of pieces. We have printed the foundation patterns you need for the 5"-tall letters in Liz's alphabet quilt and 2½"-tall letters in Marianne's quilt. The foundation patterns are reversed so the letters and numbers will read correctly when pieced.

1. Using ruler and pencil, trace the outline of all shapes and the outer edge of the foundation pattern onto tracing paper. Lightly shade the shaded portion

of the foundation on your paper and number the pieces. The numbers indicate the order you will stitch pieces to the foundation.

2. Using fabric scraps that are larger than numbered sections, place fabrics for sections 1 and 2 right sides together. Position paper pattern atop fabrics with printed side facing you. Make sure the fabric for section 1 is under that section and that edges of fabrics extend ¼" beyond sewing line between the two sections.

3. Using a short machine stitch so that papers will tear off easily later, sew along stitching line between the two sections, extending stitching into seam allowances at ends of seams.

4. Open out pieces and finger press seam.

5. Place the next piece right sides together with the #2 piece, making sure that ¼" extends beyond the stitching line for seam allowance. Stitch along the stitching line between #2 and #3. Open out #3 piece and finger press seam. Continue to add pieces in numerical order, placing fabric pieces right sides together, until foundation is covered.

6. When all numbered sections of foundation are covered, work from paper side and use rotary cutter and ruler to trim excess paper and fabric along outer lines of pattern.

7. Carefully tear off foundation paper.

8. Use diagonal seams method or traditional piecing as needed to complete letter.

GRAPHED NUMBERS

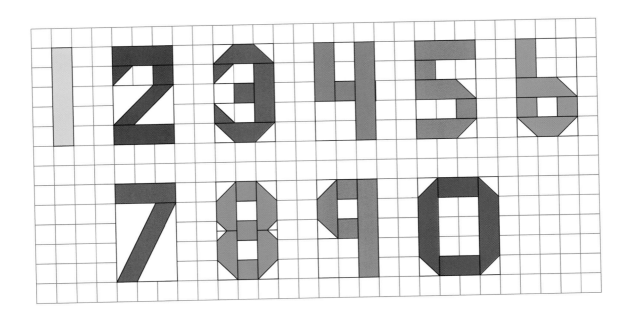

GRAPHED LETTERS

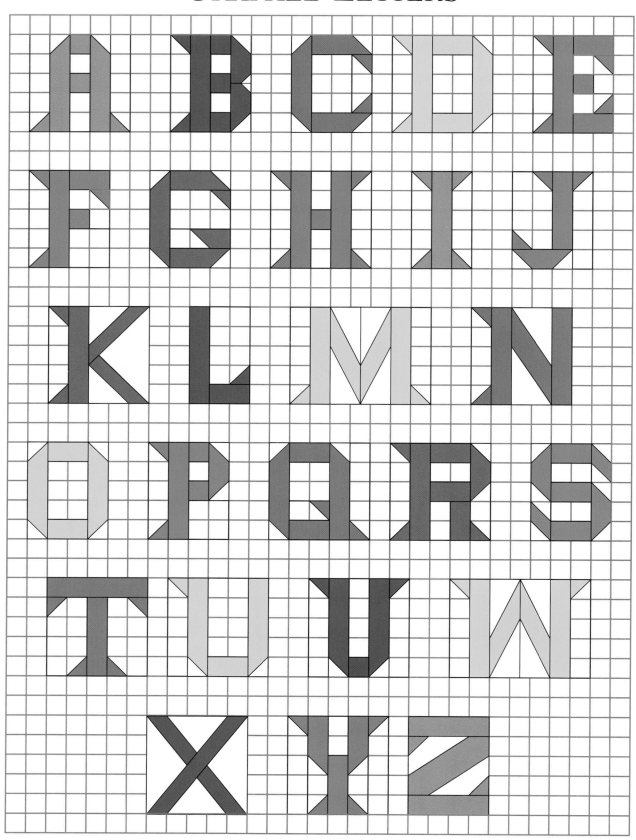

FOUNDATIONS FOR 5"-TALL LETTERS AND NUMBERS

(GRID IS 1")

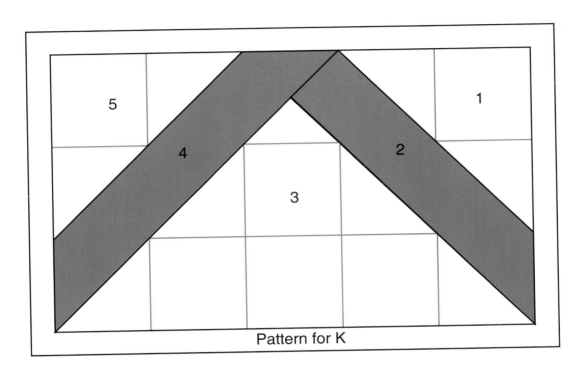

Pattern for K

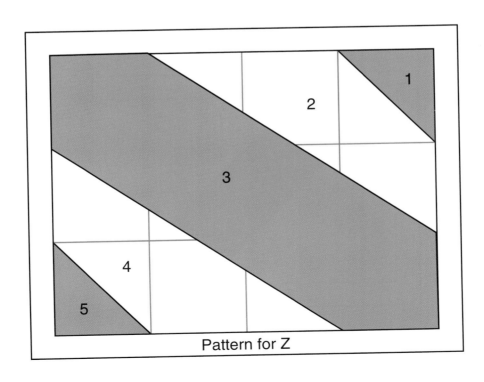

Pattern for Z

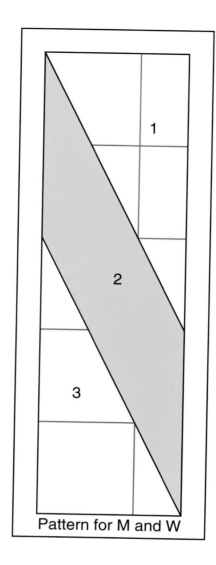

Pattern for M and W

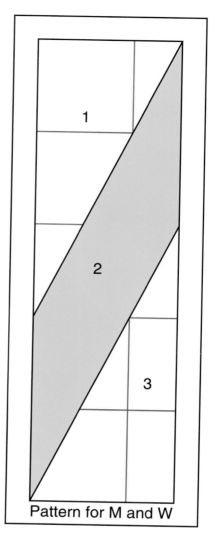

Pattern for M and W

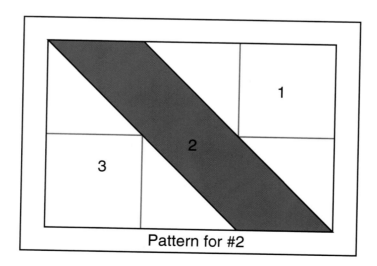

Pattern for #2

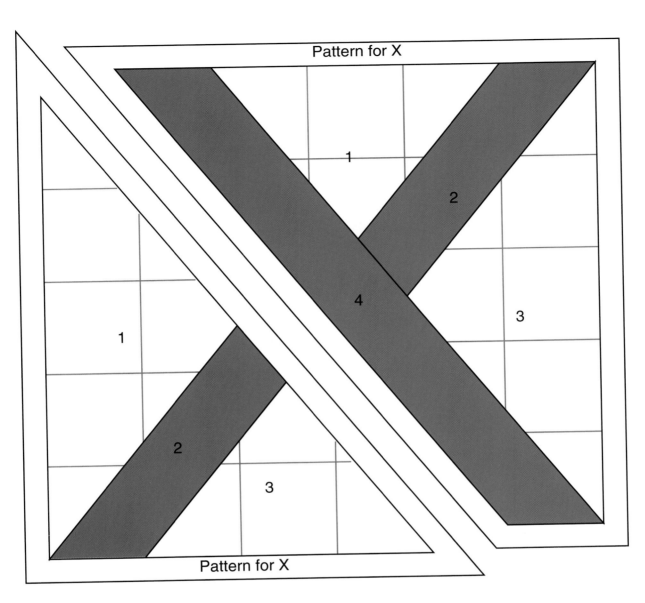

Pattern for X

Pattern for X

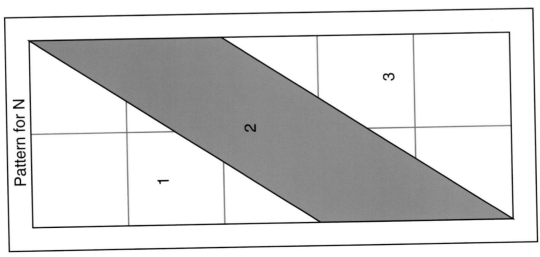

Pattern for N

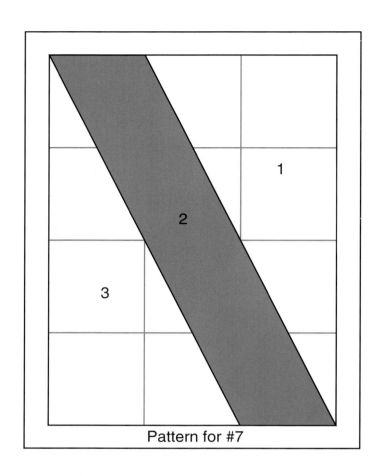

Pattern for #7

FOUNDATIONS FOR 2½"-TALL LETTERS AND NUMBERS

(GRID IS ½")

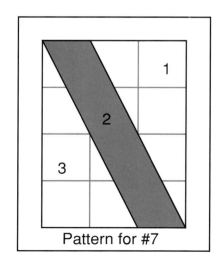

Pattern for #7

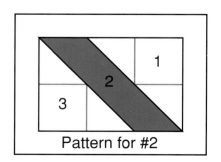

Pattern for #2

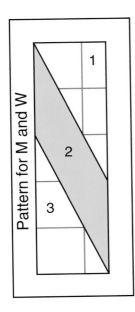

Pattern for M and W

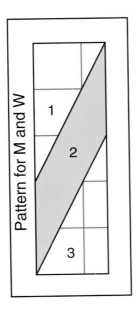

Pattern for M and W

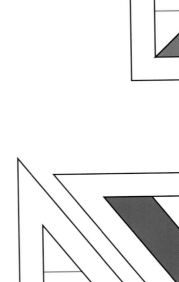

Pattern for K

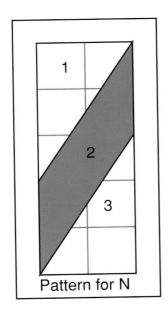

Pattern for N

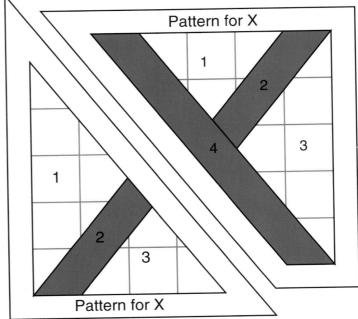

Pattern for X

Pattern for X

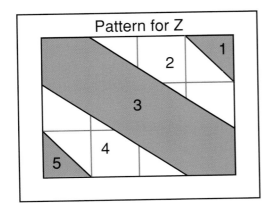

Pattern for Z

ALPHABET MINI QUILT

Marianne chose small-scale reproduction prints to give her miniature alphabet quilt the look of a 19th century quilt. The colored fabric letters stand out boldly against the light shirting print background fabric.

Machine pieced
and machine quilted by
Marianne Fons

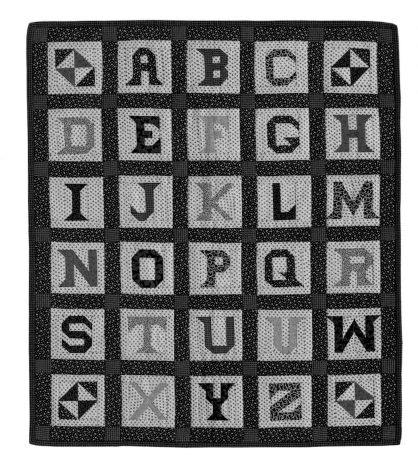

Finished size 23½" x 28"
Blocks 26 (3½") Letter blocks and
4 (3½") Broken Dishes blocks

MATERIALS

❏ ½ yard of black print fabric for sashing, Broken Dishes blocks, and A, G, and Q letters

❏ ⅓ yard of red-and-black check fabric for sashing squares, binding, and B, J, and U letters

❏ 1¼ yards of cream shirting print for Broken Dishes blocks, background of all letter blocks, and framing strips for all blocks

❏ Fat eighth* yard of green print fabric for C, M, P, and Z letters

❏ Fat eighth* yard of cheddar yellow print fabric for D, K, R, and T letters

❏ Fat eighth* yard of blue print #1 fabric for Broken Dishes blocks and I, L, and S letters

❏ Fat eighth* yard of blue print #2 fabric for E, O, W, and Y letters

❏ Fat eighth* yard of pink print fabric for F, V, and X letters

❏ Fat eighth* yard of red print fabric for Broken Dishes blocks and H and N letters

❏ ¾ yard fabric for quilt back

❏ 25" x 30" rectangle of quilt batting

Fat eighth = 9" x 22"

CUTTING

Measurements include ¼" seam allowances. Cut strips across fabric width. Refer to graphed letters on page 10 to cut pieces for letters. Each square on graph will equal ½" to make letters that finish 2½" tall before framing. (See Patchwork Alphabets on pages 6-9.)

From black print fabric, cut:

■ 8 (1½"-wide) strips. From these, cut 71 (1½" x 4") sashing rectangles.

■ 4 (2⅛") squares. Cut each square in half diagonally to make a total of 8 half-square triangles for Broken Dishes blocks.
■ Pieces for A, G, and Q letters.

From red and black check fabric, cut:
■ 2 (1½"-wide) strips. From these, cut 42 (1½") sashing squares.
■ 3 (2¼"-wide) strips for binding.
■ Pieces for B, J, and U letters.

From shirting print fabric, cut:
■ 1 (2⅛"-wide) strip. From this, cut 8 (2⅛") squares. Cut each square in half diagonally to make 16 half-square triangles for Broken Dishes blocks.
■ 7 (1"-wide) strips. From these, cut 60 (1" x 4") rectangles for framing tops and bottoms of all blocks and 8 (1" x 3") rectangles for framing sides of Broken Dishes blocks.
■ Background pieces for letters by referring to letter charts on page 10.
■ Side framing strips for letter blocks as needed.

From green print fabric, cut:
■ Pieces for C, M, P, and Z letters.

From cheddar yellow print fabric, cut:
■ Pieces for D, K, R, and T letters.

From blue print #1 fabric, cut:
■ 2 (2⅛") squares. Cut each square in half diagonally to make 4 half-square triangles for Broken Dishes blocks.
■ Pieces for I, L, and S letters.

From blue print #2 fabric, cut:
■ Pieces for E, O, W, and Y letters.

From pink print fabric, cut:
■ Pieces for F, V, and X letters.

From red print fabric, cut:
■ 2 (2⅛") squares. Cut each square in half diagonally to make 4 half-square triangles for Broken Dishes blocks.
■ Pieces for H and N letters.

BROKEN DISHES ASSEMBLY

1. Referring to *Block Assembly Diagram,* join black print and shirting print triangles to make 8 triangle-square units. Make 4 red/shirting triangle-square units and 4 blue/shirting print triangle-square units.

Block Assembly Diagram   *Block Diagram*

2. Join 2 red/shirting and 2 black/shirting triangle-square units as shown. Make 2 blocks of this type and 2 with blue/shirting units.
3. Join 1" x 3" strips to sides of blocks. Join 1" x 4" strips to top and bottom edges of blocks.

LETTER BLOCK ASSEMBLY

1. Assemble letters using either diagonal seams, foundation piecing, or a combination of techniques.
2. From shirting print fabric, cut and sew strips to add to sides of letters to make blocks measure 4" wide. Sew 1" x 4" strips to top and bottom of blocks so blocks are 4" square and will finish 3½" square.

QUILT ASSEMBLY

1. Referring to photograph on page 16, lay out blocks, sashing strips, and sashing squares.
2. Join pieces into rows; join rows.

FINISHING

1. Mark quilting designs as desired.
2. Layer quilt back, batting, and quilt top; baste.
3. Quilt as desired. Quilt shown was machine quilted in-the-ditch.

LADY OF THE LAKE QUILT

To celebrate her son Jacob's graduation from the U. S. Naval Academy and his commissioning as a naval officer, Liz made this quilt with signatures and well wishes of family and friends. To make the quilt extra special, Liz pieced letters and numbers for the border. The Lady of the Lake blocks and assorted blue fabrics set the nautical theme.

Finished size   89" x 105"
Blocks   63 (8") blocks

MATERIALS

❏ 32 fat eighths* of assorted blue print fabrics for blocks and border triangles
❏ ½ yard each of 4 navy print fabrics for blocks and border letters and numbers
❏ 2¾ yards of navy print fabric for outer border and binding
❏ 7 yards of tea-dye solid fabric for blocks and borders
❏ 8¼ yards of fabric for quilt back
❏ King-size quilt batting
Fat eighth = 9" x 22"

CUTTING

Measurements include ¼" seam allowances. Cut strips across fabric width unless directed otherwise. Instructions for cutting letters, numbers, and middle borders are listed separately from these general quilt cutting instructions.

From each assorted blue fat eighth, cut:
■ 1 (6⅞") square. Cut square in half diagonally to make 2 half-square A triangles. You will have a total of 63 triangles for quilt and 1 extra triangle.
■ 8 (2⅞") squares. Cut each square in half diagonally to make 2 half-square B triangles. You will have 512 triangles total.

From each of 4 navy print fabrics, cut:
■ 2 (2⅞"-wide) strips. From these, cut 21 (2⅞") squares from each pair of strips. Cut each square in half diagonally to make 2 half-square B triangles. You will have a total of 168 triangles.
■ Reserve remaining fabrics for border letters.

From navy print outer border fabric, cut:
■ 2 (6" x 94½") **lengthwise** side borders.
■ 2 (6" x 89½") **lengthwise** end borders.
■ 4 (2¼" x 98") **lengthwise** binding strips.

From tea-dye solid fabric, cut:
■ 6 (6⅞"-wide) strips. From these, cut 32 (6⅞") squares. Cut each square in half diagonally to make 2 half-square A triangles. You will have 1 extra triangle.
■ 26 (2⅞"-wide) strips. From these, cut 337 (2⅞") squares. Cut each square in half diagonally to make 2 half-square B triangles.
■ Reserve remaining fabric for letters and borders.

Designed and pieced by Liz Porter

Hand quilted by Ada Troyer, Vera Troyer

Katie Troyer and Mary Yoder

WRITING ON FABRIC

Quilters have been writing their names and also special messages on fabric since the mid-1830s, when an indelible ink that didn't rot fabric was developed.

We write on fabric to collect signatures and special messages for commemorative or friendship quilts. You can also write on fabric to make a signature label for the back of a quilt. Record all the pertinent data about the quilt on its label, such as date made, maker, recipient, fabrics used, etc.

When choosing pens for signatures, be sure to use only those designed specifically for writing on fabric. Popular brands currently available are Gelly Roll and Pigma® pens. The Gelly Roll pens are available in many pretty colors. Pigma pens area available in several colors and also several point thicknesses.

You will also need freezer paper from the grocery store to stabilize signature areas.

INSTRUCTIONS

1. Cut out pieces for the signature areas of your quilt. Choose light value, relatively plain fabrics so the writing will show up well.

2. Cut out freezer paper pieces. Make paper pieces "finished size," i.e., without seam allowances.

3. Press shiny side of freezer paper pieces to wrong side of fabric. Use a dry iron set at wool.

4. Use a pen designed especially for writing on fabric. Write on the right side of the fabric piece. Write only on the area that has paper behind it.

5. Turn fabric piece to wrong side and carefully peel off freezer paper. Freezer paper pieces can be reused until they lose their "stick."

6. Heat set signatures by pressing with a dry iron set at cotton.

BLOCK UNIT ASSEMBLY

If desired, obtain signatures of family and friends on tea-dye A triangles before assembling blocks. (See Organizing A Signature Quilt on page 23.)

1. Join 1 blue A triangle to 1 tea-dye A triangle to make triangle-square unit. Repeat to make 63 A triangle-square units.

2. Join 1 blue B triangle to 1 tea-dye B triangle to make triangle-square unit. Repeat to make 674 B triangle-square units. You will have a few extra blue B triangles.

3. Referring to *Block Assembly Diagram,* join 3 assorted B triangle-square units into a strip for right side of block. Pay attention to angle of triangle-square unit seams. Make 63 strips of 3 B units.

4. Referring to *Block Assembly Diagram,* join 4 assorted B triangle-square units into a strip for top of block. Pay attention to angle of triangle-square unit seams. Make 63 strips of 4 B units.

BLOCK ASSEMBLY

1. Referring to *Block Assembly Diagram,* lay out 1 A unit, 1 strip of 3 B units, and 1 strip of 4 B units as shown. Join strip of 3 B units to right side of A unit. Join strip of 4 B units to top edge of block as shown in *Block Diagram.*

2. Make 63 Lady of the Lake blocks.

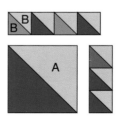

Block Assembly Diagram

Block Diagram

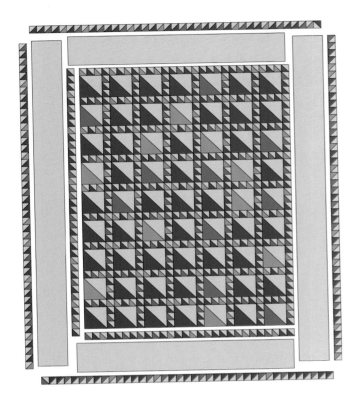

Quilt Assembly Diagram

INNER QUILT ASSEMBLY

1. Referring to *Quilt Assembly Diagram,* join blocks in 9 horizontal rows with 7 blocks in each row. Join rows.

2. Join 28 B triangle-square units to make strip to finish bottom edge of quilt. Pay attention to angle of triangle-square unit seams. Sew strip to bottom edge of quilt.

3. Join 37 B triangle-square units to make strip to finish left side of quilt. Pay attention to angle of triangle-square unit seams. Sew strip to left side of quilt.

LETTER AND NUMBER BORDER ASSEMBLY

Charts for letters and numbers are on pages 9-10. Instructions for making letters and numbers are on pages 6-9.

1. Make 5" tall finished letters and numbers as desired. Liz used a different navy print for the words on each side of her quilt.

2. Arrange letters and numbers to form words and date. From tea-dye solid fabric, cut 1½" x 5½" strips to use as spacers between letters or numbers and 2½" x 5½" strips to use as spacers between words as needed. Join letters to make words.

3. From tea-dye solid fabric, cut 2"-wide strips as needed to use as spacers for top and bottom of words. Measure length of each word unit. Piece 2"-wide strips to length. Join strips to top and bottom of words so word units are 8½" tall, including seam allowances.

4. From tea-dye solid, cut 8½"-wide strips as needed to add to ends of word units to complete letter borders. Join word units and 8½"-wide tea-dye strips to make 2 (58½"-long) borders for top and bottom edges of quilt. Join borders to quilt. Join word units and 8½"-wide tea-dye strips to make 2 (90½"-long) borders for quilt sides. Join borders to quilt.

OUTER PIECED BORDER ASSEMBLY

1. Referring to *Quilt Assembly Diagram,* join 45 B triangle-square units to make border for right side of quilt. Pay attention to angle of triangle-square unit seams. Join border to quilt. Repeat for left side border.

2. Join 39 B triangle-square units to make top border. Pay careful attention to angle of triangle-square unit seams. Join border to top edge of quilt. Repeat for bottom border.

3. Join 6" x 94½" navy blue borders to sides of quilt. Join 6" x 89½" borders to top and bottom edges.

FINISHING

1. Mark quilting designs as desired. The quilt shown is hand quilted with diagonal lines across the large blue triangles and outline quilting around the small blue triangles. All pieced letters are outline quilted with a diagonal grid of 1" squares in the background around the letters. The corners of the light border feature a quilted anchor surrounded by clamshell quilting. A pattern for the clamshell quilting design is below. The navy borders have a dolphin quilted in each corner with rope quilting along the lengths of the borders. The rope quilting design is below.

2. Divide backing fabric into 3 (2¾-yard) pieces. Join panels. Seams on quilt back will run parallel to top edge of quilt.
3. Layer quilt back, batting, and quilt top; baste.
4. Quilt as desired.

Clamshell Quilting Design

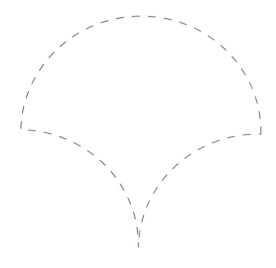

Clamshell Quilting Design Pattern

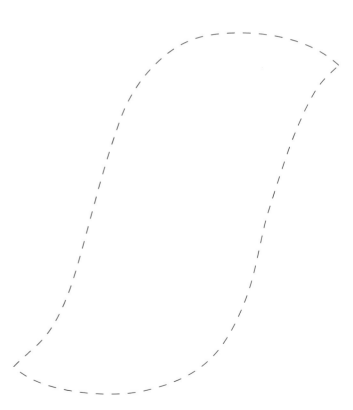

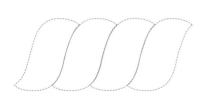

Rope Quilting Design

Rope Quilting Design Pattern

ORGANIZING A SIGNATURE QUILT

Quilts with signatures and messages have a long history in American quilt making, and we like carrying on that tradition. The spectacular Lady of the Lake quilt Liz made for her son Jacob's graduation from the U.S. Naval Academy was a perfect memento to cap his four years at Annapolis.

Organizing and completing a special quilt like this takes careful planning. Most important is allowing a realistic amount of time. Start thinking about that quilt in the fall of your son or daughter's senior year! Here are our suggestions and a timeline for a successful signature quilt project.

SUGGESTIONS

■ Choose a patchwork block that has a good area for signatures. Ideal is a pattern that has a patchwork area you can construct while you wait to get signature pieces back. Plan on leaving some signature areas blank to write on later.

■ Be sure to select a light value fabric for the signature area so names and messages will show up well.

■ Allow approximately 12 weeks from start to finish, even longer if you are planning on hand quilting. Make a written schedule and stick to it.

TIMELINE

Week 1
■ Plan your quilt.
■ Purchase fabrics and special pens for signatures. Buy lots of pens to send out with fabric pieces—many people probably won't remember to send them back.

Week 2
■ Prepare signature areas for signing (See Writing on Fabric, page 20.)
■ Write out instructions for signing and include the instructions when you send out pieces.
■ Make a written list with addresses and phone

numbers of people whose signatures you want. You may need to enlist the help of one of your child's school friends and/or work friends to help you make your list. Swear these helpers to secrecy!

■ Mail prepared fabric pieces, pens, stamped return envelopes, and instructions to distant friends and family and local people. Give them a deadline for returning signatures. Set yourself a deadline to make reminder calls.

■ If you aren't planning to do the quilting yourself, line up a machine quilter or hand quilter. Give your quilter a date you will be delivering the top and a date you need it quilted by.

Week 3
■ Cut out and work on other parts of the quilt. For Jacob's quilt, Liz was able to cut out and stitch the many small half-square triangles for the blocks while she was waiting for the signature pieces to come back.

Week 4
■ Start calling people to remind them to return their signed pieces.
■ Keep sewing other sections of the quilt.

Weeks 5 & 6
■ As signatures arrive, remove freezer paper and heat set signatures by pressing with a hot iron (no steam).
■ Make final phone calls to get in all the signatures.
■ Assemble blocks.

Weeks 7 & 8
■ Set quilt together and mark quilting designs.

Week 9 to final week
■ Get busy quilting or take quilt to quilter.
■ Make binding and label for back of quilt.
■ Find a big box and buy wrapping paper.

Final Week
■ Stitch binding to quilt and finish.
■ Sew label to back of quilt.
■ Present the quilt. Have Kleenex® handy.

S A V A N N A H
P I N W H E E L
Q U I L T

Marianne captured the look of an early American quilt by using simple blocks set with a medium to large scale floral print fabric. She used pre-1850 reproduction fabrics from Savannah by Fons & Porter for Benartex.

Machine pieced by
M A R I A N N E   F O N S
Machine quilted by
L Y N N   W I T Z E N B U R G

Finished size   33½" x 42"
Blocks   12 (6") blocks

M A T E R I A L S

❑ 1 yard of brown large floral print fabric for blocks, borders, and binding
❑ ½ yard of small floral print fabric for setting squares and triangles
❑ 4 fat eighths* of assorted blue print fabrics
❑ 3 fat eighths* of assorted brown print fabrics
❑ 1 yard of fabric for quilt back
❑ Crib-size quilt batting
Fat eighth = 9" x 22"

C U T T I N G

Measurements include ¼" seam allowance. Cut strips crosswise.

From brown large floral print fabric, cut:
■ 4 (4½"-wide) strips for borders. Trim 2 strips to 34½" long for side borders and 2 strips to 34" long for top and bottom borders.
■ 4 (2½"-wide) strips for binding.
■ 1 (3⅞"-wide) strip. From this, cut 6 (3⅞") squares. Cut each square in half diagonally to make 12 triangles.

From small floral print fabric, cut:

■ 1 (6½"-wide) strip. From this, cut 6 (6½") setting squares.

■ 1 (9¾"-wide) strip. From this, cut:

■ 3 (9¾") squares. Cut each square in quarters diagonally to make 12 side setting triangles. You will have 2 extra.

■ 2 (5¼") squares. Cut squares in half diagonally to make 4 corner setting triangles.

From each fat eighth, cut:

■ 6 (3⅞") squares. Cut each in half diagonally to make 12 triangles of each fabric.

BLOCK ASSEMBLY

1. Join 1 blue triangle to 1 brown triangle to make triangle-square unit. Repeat to make a total of 12 matching triangle-square units.

2. Referring to *Block Assembly Diagram,* join 4 triangle-squares to make block as shown in *Block Diagram.* Repeat to make 3 matching blocks.

3. Repeat Steps 1 and 2 to make a total of 12 blocks.

Block Assembly Diagram   *Block Diagram*

QUILT ASSEMBLY

1. Referring to *Quilt Assembly Diagram,* lay out blocks, setting squares, and setting triangles.

2. Join blocks and setting pieces in diagonal rows. Join rows.

3. Join side borders to quilt sides. Join end borders to top and bottom edges.

4. Quilt as desired. Quilt shown has spider web motifs in setting pieces and straight lines in blocks. Borders have meandering feather design.

Quilt Assembly Diagram

CHARACTERISTICS OF EARLY AMERICAN FABRICS & QUILTS

Before 1800, quilts were rare and expensive in America—printed cloth was a luxury. Early nineteenth century designs were printed on cloth by hand with wood blocks, copper plates, copper rollers, and brushes.

After 1776, Americans began to produce cotton cloth domestically, and cotton became cheaper than imported goods. Cotton became the signature fabric for the American quilt.

Pre-1850 fabric designs were often large-scale, multicolored, and elaborate. Block printed designs included striped and trailing florals, game birds, palm trees, and "pillar prints" with flowers or drapes at the top of the fake architectural columns. Early copper rollers produced multicolored "rainbow" stripes, sometimes with other motifs printed atop them. Other types of copper roller prints were fancy "machine grounds"—backgrounds of tiny dots, worm-like squiggles, fine honeycombs, and "cracked ice." Printed atop these grounds were floral sprays, curly leaves with tattered edges, sprigs with berries, and jagged-edge geometrics.

Between 1800 and 1850, dyes were primarily vegetable or mineral natural dyes. The first synthetic dyes were invented in 1856. Colors for pre-1850 fabrics include Prussian blue, indigo, soft teal, turquoise, light blue, lapis blue, Turkey red, brick, rose, plum, buttercup yellow, butterscotch yellow, bright "cheddar" orange, and many shades of green and brown.

Many fabric companies are printing reproductions of early 19th century fabrics. Pictured here are a few examples of new fabrics inspired by old ones.

Medallion-style quilts were gradually replaced in popularity by the typical American block-style layout. Pieced patterns started out simple but became more complicated. Quilters invented their own appliqué designs, reaching a zenith of complexity with the famous album quilts of Baltimore in the 1850s.

USING A SPECIAL RULER TO CUT HALF-SQUARE TRIANGLES

When blocks call for squares and triangle-square units that finish the same size, you can use a special triangle ruler that lets you cut both kinds of units from the same strip. Both the EZAngle™ ruler and the Omnigrid® #96 ruler are triangular rulers designed to cut half-square triangles from strips ½" larger, instead of ⅞" larger, than the desired finished size of the triangle. We almost always use this method when cutting half-square triangles.

1. Begin by cutting a strip ½" wider than the desired finished size of the square. For example, for a 3" finished square, cut a 3½"-wide strip.

2. Cut as many squares as you need for your design.

3. To cut the half-square triangles, place the special triangle ruler atop the strip. If you are using an EZAngle™ align the blunted end with the top edge of the fabric strip. If you are using an Omnigrid® triangle, align the dashed line inset from the point of the triangle even with the top edge of the fabric strip as shown in *Diagram 1*.

Diagram 1

Cut along the slanted edge of the ruler. Your triangle will have one blunted corner as shown in *Diagram 2*. (We know these triangles look funny, but they work just like triangles cut traditionally. All you are missing on the blunted edge is the little triangle tip that you usually trim off after triangles are joined into a triangle-square unit. Triangles cut in this manner only need to be trimmed on one end!)

Diagram 2

4. Rotate the ruler as shown in *Diagram 3* and cut another triangle along the ruler's straight edge.

Diagram 3

5. Continue cutting triangles from the strip as shown in *Diagram 4* until you have the needed number of triangles.

Diagram 4

6. When joining triangles cut this way into triangle-square units, place triangles right sides together, matching blunted ends as shown in *Diagram 5*.

Diagram 5

7. Press the seam allowances toward the darker fabric. Trim the excess triangle tips from the one end as shown in *Diagram 6*.

Diagram 6

PLANTATION STAR QUILT

Liz played with shading square-in-a-square units to devise this star pattern. She used fabrics from our own Savannah collection for Benartex® to give the quilt an early 19th century feel. Liz says, "I think the green sashing strips and border fabrics look a bit like the Spanish moss that drapes many live oak trees on plantations in the south."

Finished size   77½" x 93"
Blocks   20 (12") blocks

MATERIALS

❑ ⅓ yard each of 20 assorted medium/dark print fabrics for blocks
❑ 10 fat eighths* of assorted light print fabrics for block backgrounds
❑ 2 yards of olive green stripe fabric for sashing and binding
❑ ¼ yard of brown print fabric for sashing squares
❑ 2⅓ yards of olive green large-scale bird print fabric for borders
❑ 6 yards of 45"-wide fabric or 3 yards of 90" or wider fabric for quilt back
❑ Queen-size quilt batting
Fat eighth = 9" x 22"

CUTTING

Measurements include ¼" seam allowances. Cut all strips across the fabric width unless directed otherwise.

From each medium/dark fabric, cut:
■ 1 (4½"-wide) strip. From this cut 5 (4½") A squares and 4 (4½") C squares.

■ 2 (2½"-wide) strips. From these, cut 16 (2½") B squares and 4 (2½") D squares.

From each light fabric, cut:
■ 3 (2½" x 22") strips. From these, cut 24 (2½") E squares.

From olive stripe, cut:
■ 11 (4"-wide) strips. From these, cut 31 (4" x 12½") rectangles for sashing strips.
■ 9 (2¼"-wide) strips for binding.

From brown print, cut:
■ 2 (4"-wide) strips. From these, cut 12 (4") sashing squares.

From large-scale bird print, cut:
■ 4 (10" x 84") **lengthwise** border strips.

Designed and pieced by   Liz Porter
Machine quilted by   Kelly Ashton

BLOCK ASSEMBLY

1. To make 1 block, choose 1 matching set of 5 (4½") A squares and 16 (2½") B squares for center star and matching pieces. Choose 1 matching set of 4 (4½") C squares and 4 (2½") D squares from a second fabric. Choose 12 matching (2½") E squares from 1 light fabric for block background.

2. Referring to *Center Side Unit Diagonal Seams Diagrams,* place 2½" B squares atop opposite corners of 1 (4½") C square. Stitch diagonally as shown. (See Diagonal Seams Patchwork, page 3.) Trim 1/4" beyond stitching, open out triangle, and press. Repeat for remaining 2 corners. Make 4 Center Side Units.

Center Side Unit Diagonal Seams Diagrams

3. Referring to *Corner Unit Diagonal Seams Diagrams,* place 1 (2½") light E square and 1 (2½") D square atop opposite corners of 1 (4½") A square. Stitch diagonally, trim, open out, and press. Place E squares atop remaining corners of A square. Stitch diagonally, trim, open out, and press. Make 4 Corner Units.

Corner Unit Diagonal Seams Diagrams

4. Referring to *Block Assembly Diagram,* lay out 4 Center Side Units, 4 Corner Units, and 1 (4½") A square as shown. Join units in three rows; join rows to complete block. Make 20 Plantation Star blocks as shown in *Block Diagram.*

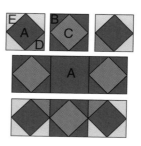 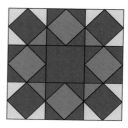

Block Assembly Diagram   *Block Diagram*

QUILT ASSEMBLY

1. Referring to photograph, join 4 blocks and 3 sashing strips to make 1 block row. Make 5 block rows. (For a quicker, easier method of quilt assembly, see Pre-sashing Blocks for Quicker Setting on page 57.)

2. Join 4 sashing strips and 3 sashing squares to make sashing row. Make 4 sashing rows.

3. Join block and sashing rows, alternating types.

4. Measure quilt length and trim 2 border strips to this measurement (approximately 74½" long). Sew borders to quilt sides.

5. Measure quilt width, including side borders, and trim remaining border strips to this measurement (approximately 78" long). Sew borders to top and bottom edges of quilt top.

FINISHING

1. Mark quilting designs as desired.

2. Divide backing fabric into 2 (3-yard) pieces. Divide 1 panel in half lengthwise. Join 1 half panel to each side of wide panel. Press seam allowances toward narrow panels.

3. Layer quilt back, batting, and quilt top; baste.

4. Quilt as desired.

JULY 4TH MINI QUILT

Liz used small Three-and-Six blocks for her quick patriotic mini quilt. She "fussy cut" the flag print fabric to position a tiny flag in the center of each block.

Machine pieced and quilted by
Liz Porter

Finished size   13½" x 17¾"
Blocks   6 (3") blocks

MATERIALS

❏ 6 scraps (at least 2" x 6") of red print fabrics for blocks
❏ Scrap (at least 1½" x 10") of tan flag print for block center squares
❏ Fat eighth* of tan solid fabric for block backgrounds
❏ Fat eighth* of first navy star print fabric for setting squares and triangles
❏ Fat eighth* of red and tan stripe fabric for inner border
❏ Fat quarter** of second navy star print fabric for outer border and binding
❏ Fat quarter** of fabric for quilt back

❏ 15" x 19" piece of quilt batting
Fat eighth = 9" x 22"
**Fat quarter = 18" x 22"*

CUTTING

Measurements include ¼" seam allowances.

From each red print fabric, cut:
■ 3 (1⅞") squares. Cut each square in half diagonally to make 2 A half-square triangles. You will have 6 sets of 6 A half-square triangles.

From tan flag fabric, cut:
■ 6 (1½") B squares.

From tan solid fabric, cut:
■ 1 (1½" x 22") strip. From this, cut 12 (1½") B squares.

- 2 (1⅞" x 22") strips. From these, cut 18 (1⅞") squares. Cut each square in half diagonally to make 2 A half-square triangles. You will have 36 A triangles.

From first navy star print fabric, cut:
- 2 (5½") squares. Cut each square in quarters diagonally to make 8 quarter-square triangles for side setting triangles. You will have 2 extra.
- 2 (3½") setting squares.
- 2 (3") squares. Cut each square in half diagonally to make 4 half-square corner setting triangles.

From red and tan stripe fabric, cut:
- 3 (1" x 22") strips. From these, cut 2 (1" x 13¼") side borders and 2 (1" x 10") end borders.

From second navy star print fabric, cut:
- 4 (2½" x 18") strips. From these, cut 2 (2½" x 14¼") side borders and 2 (2½" x 14") end borders.
- 4 (2¼" x 18") strips for binding.

BLOCK ASSEMBLY

1. Join 1 red A triangle to 1 tan A triangle to make triangle-square unit. Repeat to make triangle-square units from all red triangles and tan solid triangles.
2. Referring to *Block Assembly Diagram,* lay out 6 matching triangle-square units, 1 flag print B center square, and 2 tan print B squares. Join pieces into 3 rows. Join rows to complete block as shown in *Block Diagram.*
3. Make 6 Three-and-Six blocks.

QUILT ASSEMBLY

1. Referring to *Inner Quilt Assembly Diagram,* lay out blocks, side setting triangles, corner setting triangles, and setting squares. Join pieces in diagonal rows. Press seam allowances toward setting pieces. Join rows.

Inner Quilt Assembly Diagram

2. Stitch red and tan stripe side borders to quilt sides. Stitch end borders to top and bottom edges of quilt top. Repeat for navy star borders.

FINISHING

1. Mark quilting designs as desired.
2. Layer quilt back, batting, and quilt top; baste.
3. Quilt as desired. Quilt shown was machine quilted in-the-ditch around blocks and along edges of inner borders.

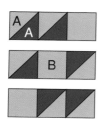

Block Assembly Diagram

Block Diagram

MAKING PATCHWORK BLOCKS A DIFFERENT SIZE

Lots of quilters are intimidated by the concept of figuring out how to cut pieces to make a block a specific size they want. Actually, it's easy to figure cutting for simple row-format blocks. Knowing how to analyse a simple block to determine the size to cut pieces is a very handy skill.

The Three-and-Six pattern is a perfect example to use for understanding simple block size changes. Look at the block diagram and notice how the block can be divided into three equal horizontal rows. Each row is made of one square and two triangle-squares. (A triangle-square is a patchwork unit made up of two half-square triangles.)

For Marianne's 9" block, each row must finish 3" (3 x 3" = 9"). For Liz's little quilt with its 3" blocks, each row must finish 1" (3 x 1" = 3").

Cutting the squares for the block is simple. All you do is add ½" to the desired finished size of the unit to include ¼-inch seam allowances. Cut the squares for Marianne's block 3½" square. Cut the squares for Liz's block 1½" square.

When cutting half-square triangles, add ⅞" to the desired finished size of the unit. For the 9" block, cut squares 3⅞" and then cut squares in half diagonally. The ⅞" takes care of the seam allowances so that when two triangle units are joined into a square the square measures 3½", including seam allowances (3" finished). For triangles for Liz's block, cut squares 1⅞" and then cut squares in half diagonally.

Just for practice, look at the block diagram again and figure the sizes to cut pieces to make a Three-and-Six block in 12" or 15" finished size.

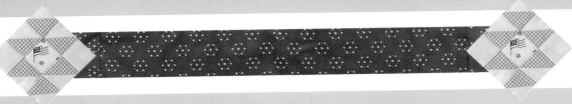

THINK ABOUT PRINT SCALE

Use medium and large scale prints for large blocks or for large patchwork units within a block to show off the print to its best advantage. Use smaller prints for the smaller units within a block. Combining different print scales within a block adds interest. If you are using all tiny prints, make small blocks or blocks with small units.

For her Southern Comfort quilt, Marianne used several medium and large scale prints. By making her Three-and-Six blocks 9" square, she was able to show off the large prints.

Liz's little July 4th Miniature uses the very same block, but in a 3" finished size. Liz made the quilt from a group of small scale patriotic prints,

perfect for the tiny units in the blocks.

Cutting up a large scale floral or other print into small squares, triangles, or other patchwork units can do a disservice to a dramatic, bold design, and can often undermine the effect of your patchwork pattern as well. For example, if you are cutting 1½" squares, one of them may fall on a large red flower and another one on a large green leaf. Your resulting block loses its continuity. The opposite pitfall is using a tiny motif in a 3" finished square. Such fabric choices often feel safe, but may turn out boring. Don't waste the opportunity to feature a gorgeous, exotic print.

SOUTHERN COMFORT QUILT

Our Savannah collection of fabrics for Benartex,® based on fabrics from before 1850, inspired this strippy set quilt. Strippy sets are a great way to feature striped fabrics, which were often used between quilt rows on early quilts. Marianne used a simple block called Three-and-Six. The block is so named because it requires just three squares and six triangle-square units.

Finished size   62¼" x 81¾"
Blocks   15 (9") blocks

MATERIALS

❑ 15 fat eighths* or scraps (at least 4½" x 15") of medium or dark print fabrics for patchwork
❑ 1 yard of light print fabric for block backgrounds
❑ ¼ yard of light print fabric for block centers
❑ 1¼ yards of print fabric for setting triangles and corner triangles
❑ 2 yards of stripe fabric for setting strips and binding
❑ 2 yards of large-scale bird print for border
❑ 5 yards of fabric for quilt back
❑ Twin-size batting
Fat eighth = 9" x 22"

CUTTING

Measurements include ¼" seam allowances. Cut all strips crosswise, unless directed otherwise.

From each dark print fabric, cut:
■ 3 (3⅞") squares. Cut squares in half diagonally to make 6 A half-square triangles.

From light print fabric for block backgrounds, cut:
■ 3 (3½"-wide) strips. Cut strips into 30 (3½") B squares.
■ 5 (3⅞"-wide) strips. Cut strips into 45 (3⅞") squares. Cut squares in half diagonally to make 90 A half-square triangles.

From light print fabric for block centers, cut:
■ 2 (3½"-wide) strips. Cut strips into 15 (3½") B squares.

From setting fabric, cut:
■ 2 (14"-wide) strips. Cut strips into 6 (14") squares. Cut squares in quarters diagonally to make 24 quarter-square X setting triangles.
■ 2 (7¼"-wide) strips. Cut strips into 6 (7¼") squares. Cut squares in half diagonally to make 12 half-square Z setting triangles.

From stripe fabric, cut:
■ 2 (3½" x 72") **lengthwise** strips.
■ 10 (2¼" x 35") crosswise strips for binding.

From border fabric, cut:
■ 4 (9½" x 66") **lengthwise** strips for borders, centering bird motifs in strips.

Designed and pieced by   Marianne Fons
Machine quilted by   Kelly Ashton

BLOCK ASSEMBLY

1. Join 1 dark and 1 light print triangle to form 1 triangle-square unit. Repeat to make 15 sets of 6 matching triangle-square units.

2. Referring to *Block Assembly Diagram,* lay out light print squares, 6 matching triangle-square units, and 1 center square as shown. Join units to form rows. Press seam allowances in opposite directions. Join rows to make block as shown in *Block Diagram.*

3. Repeat to make 15 Three-and-Six blocks.

Block Assembly Diagram   *Block Diagram*

QUILT ASSEMBLY

1. Referring to photograph, lay out blocks, X setting triangles, and Z corner triangles to form 3 vertical rows with 5 blocks in each row.

2. Referring to *Row Piecing Diagram,* join blocks and setting pieces. Trim outside edges of setting pieces as needed, making sure to allow ¼" seam allowance at block corners.

3. Measure length of row. Trim 3½"-wide stripe strips to this length (approximately 64"). Join block rows and strips, alternating rows and strips as shown in photograph on page 35. (See Strippy Sets, page 37.)

4. Trim 2 wide border strips to same length as stripe strips. Add borders to opposite sides of quilt top.

5. Measure width of quilt top, including borders. Trim 2 borders to this length (approximately 62½"). Add borders to top and bottom of quilt top.

FINISHING

1. Divide backing fabric into two 2½-yard lengths. Divide one piece in half lengthwise. Join narrow panels to sides of wide panel. Press seam allowances toward narrow panels.

2. Layer backing, batting, and quilt top; baste.

3. Quilt as desired. The quilt shown was machine quilted with vertical lines spaced about 1" apart in the blocks and horizontal lines spaced about 2" apart in the setting and corner triangles. The strips separating the rows of block are quilted in a diamond pattern. The outer borders are quilted in a meander pattern that emphasizes the bird motifs in the fabric.

Row Piecing Diagram

A strippy set is a quilt layout that has vertical rows of patchwork alternated with fabric strips. This type of setting is of British origin and was fashionable with American quilters early in the 19th century. A strippy set quilt that has enjoyed continued popularity is the Goose Chase design with its alternate rows of small Goose Chase units and fabric strips.

Marianne's Southern Comfort quilt is an example of a strippy set. She arranged her patchwork blocks in vertical rows, turning them on point and squaring them off with a beige fabric. She separated the rows with long strips of a striped fabric. All the fabrics are from our Savannah collection for Benartex®.

When joining rows of patchwork blocks in this fashion, be sure the blocks are lined up evenly across the width of the quilt. If they aren't lined up, they can look like they've slid one way or the other–the blocks stair-step instead of being properly aligned.

To keep blocks aligned, begin by stitching the first unpieced fabric strip to the right hand side of the left vertical row of blocks. Then, working on the wrong side of the fabric, use a ruler and pencil to mark horizontal lines across the unpieced spacer strip at the corner point of each block. When you join the next row (the middle one for Marianne's quilt), match the corners of the blocks on the new row to the pencil marks on the unpieced spacer strip as shown in *Alignment Diagram*.

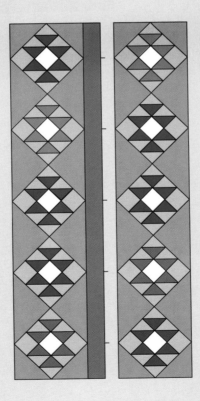

Alignment Diagram

ALBUM CROSS MINI QUILT

Pink and brown was a popular color scheme for quilts in the 1870s. Liz fulfilled her desire to make a quilt in this color scheme with her quick and easy Album Cross Mini Quilt.

Machine pieced and machine quilted by Liz Porter

Finished size   13" x 17"
Blocks   12 (3") blocks

MATERIALS

❏ 6 scraps (at least 6" x 6") of assorted brown print fabrics for blocks

❏ 6 scraps (at least 6" x 6") of assorted pink print fabrics for blocks

❏ Scrap (at least 1½" x 21") of tan solid fabric for block centers

❏ Fat eighth* of pink print fabric for sashing squares

❏ ⅓ yard of brown print fabric for sashing strips and binding

❏ Fat quarter** of fabric for quilt back

❏ 14" x 18" piece of quilt batting

Fat eighth = 9" x 22"

**Fat quarter = 18" x 22"*

CUTTING

Measurements include ¼" seam allowances. Cut strips crosswise. All pieces for blocks, except center squares, are cut oversized and will be trimmed to correct size and shape after block is assembled.

From each brown print and each pink print fabric scrap, cut:

■ 1 (3¼") square. Cut each square in quarters diagonally to make 4 quarter-square triangles. You will have 12 sets of 4 triangles.

■ 4 (1½" x 2½") rectangles for cross bars. You will have 12 sets of 4 rectangles.

From tan solid fabric, cut:

■ 12 (1½") squares for block centers.

From pink print fabric, cut:
- 2 (1½" x 22") strips. From these, cut 20 (1½") sashing squares.

From brown print fabric, cut:
- 3 (1½"-wide) strips. From these, cut 31 (1½" x 3½") sashing strips.
- 2 (2½"-wide) strips for binding.

BLOCK ASSEMBLY

1. Referring to *Block Assembly Diagrams,* lay out 1 set of 4 matching cross bar rectangles in one color and 1 set of 4 matching triangles in another color. You will also need 1 (1½") tan center square.

Block Assembly Diagrams

Block Diagram

2. Join cross bar rectangles to opposite sides of center square to make center bar unit. Press seam allowances toward cross bars.

3. Join triangles to opposite sides of remaining cross bar rectangles to make triangle/bar units. Press seam allowances toward cross bars. Join triangle/bar units to both sides of center unit. *Note: Points of triangles will not line up with ends of cross bar rectangles. Take care not to stretch bias edges of triangles when sewing and pressing!*

4. Make 12 Album Cross blocks.

BLOCK TRIMMING

1. Referring to *Block Trimming Diagram 1,* align 1¾" mark on ruler with opposite corners of block center square. Trim excess fabric along edge of block.

2. Rotate block 180 degrees. Align ruler with corner on center square and trim edges as shown in *Block Trimming Diagram 2.*

3. Rotate block and trim as shown in *Block Trimming Diagram 3,* making sure corner is square.

4. In a similar manner, trim the remaining side of the block so block is 3½" square as shown in *Block Diagram.* Repeat for all blocks.

Trimming Diagrams for Blocks

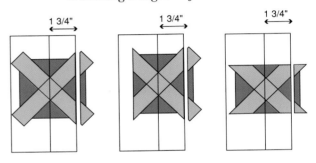

Diagram 1   Diagram 2   Diagram 3

QUILT ASSEMBLY

1. Referring to photograph, lay out blocks, sashing strips, and sashing squares. Join 4 sashing squares and 3 sashing strips to make 1 sashing row. Make 5 sashing rows. Join 3 blocks and 4 sashing strips to make 1 block row. Make 4 block rows.

2. Join sashing rows and block rows, alternating types.

FINISHING

1. Mark quilting designs as desired. Liz machine quilted in-the-ditch along the sashing strips and squares with clear monofilament thread.

2. Layer quilt back, batting, and quilt top; baste.

3. Quilt as desired.

ALBUM CROSS QUILT

As a memento of a quilting retreat, Marianne and Liz asked each participant make and sign an 8" Album Cross block. "To simplify deciding how to arrange the blocks, we just put them in alphabetical order!" Liz and Marianne then chose the sashing fabric and made the little 3" Album Cross blocks for the sashing squares. You will love the quick and easy method for assembling these blocks.

Finished size 69" x 91"
Blocks 48 (8") blocks and 63 (3") blocks

MATERIALS

❑ 3½ yards of cream shirting print fabric for sashing strips and sashing blocks
❑ ¼ yard of muslin for large block centers
❑ 50 fat eighths* of assorted medium and dark fabrics for blocks
❑ ⅔ yard of binding fabric
❑ 5½ yards of fabric for quilt back
❑ Full-size quilt batting
❑ 9" or larger square ruler
❑ 8½" x 11"-piece of typing paper
❑ Optional: fine-tip permanent marking pen for writing on fabric
❑ Optional: freezer paper
Fat eighth = 9" x 22"

CUTTING

Measurements for cutting include ¼" seam allowances. Cut all strips across fabric width. All pieces for blocks, except center squares, are cut over-sized and will be trimmed after blocks are assembled.

From cream shirting fabric, cut:
■ 28 (3½"-wide) strips. From strips, cut 110 (3½" x 8½) sashing strips.
■ 6 (3¼"-wide) strips. From strips, cut 63 (3¼") squares. Cut each square in quarters diagonally to make 252 triangles for 3" sashing blocks.

From muslin, cut:
■ 3 (2½"-wide) strips. From strips, cut 48 (2½") squares for centers of large blocks.

From assorted medium and dark print fabrics, cut:
■ 48 (7½") squares. Cut each square in quarters diagonally to make quarter-square triangles. You will have 48 sets of 4 triangles for large blocks.
■ 48 sets of 4 (2½" x 5½") rectangles for cross bars of large blocks.
■ 63 sets of 4 (1½" x 2½") rectangles for cross bars of sashing blocks.
■ 63 (1½") squares for centers of sashing blocks.

From binding fabric, cut:
■ 9 (2¼"-wide) strips.

Designed by   Liz and Marianne
Large blocks by   Participants at 1996
Fons & Porter Fall Quilt Retreat
Machine quilted by   Kathy Herzberg

LARGE BLOCK ASSEMBLY

If desired, obtain signatures of family and friends on muslin center squares before assembling blocks. (See Organizing A Signature Quilt on page 23.)

1. Referring to *Large Block Assembly Diagrams,* lay out 1 set of 4 matching large quarter-square triangles, 1 set of 4 (2½" x 5½") matching cross bar rectangles from another fabric, and 1 muslin center square.

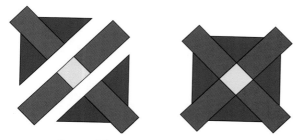

Large Block Assembly Diagrams

Large Block Diagram

2. Join cross bar rectangles to opposite sides of center square to make center bar unit. Press seam allowances toward rectangles.

3. Join triangles to opposite sides of remaining cross bar rectangles to make triangle/bar units. Press seam allowances toward cross bars. *Note: Tips of triangles will not line up with ends of cross bar rectangles. Also, take care not to stretch bias edges of triangles when sewing and pressing!*

4. Join triangle/bar units to both sides of center bar unit. Press seam allowances toward rectangles.

5. Trim block to 8½" square as explained in Trimming Album Cross Blocks on page 43.

6. Make 48 large blocks.

SASHING BLOCK ASSEMBLY

1. Lay out 4 matching cream shirting print triangles, 1 set of 4 matching 1½" x 2½" cross bar rectangles, and 1 contrasting 1½" center square. Assemble pieces in same manner as for large block.

2. Trim block as explained for blocks in Album Cross Mini Quilt on page 39. Trimmed block measures 3½" square.

3. Make 63 sashing blocks.

QUILT ASSEMBLY

1. Referring to *Quilt Assembly Diagram,* join 7 sashing squares and 6 sashing strips to make a sashing row. Press seam allowances toward sashing strips. Repeat to make a total of 9 sashing rows.

Quilt Assembly Diagram

2. Join 7 sashing strips and 6 blocks to make a block row. Press seam allowances toward sashing strips. Repeat to make a total of 8 block rows.

3. Join rows, alternating types.

1. Divide backing fabric into 2 (2¾-yard) lengths. Cut one piece in half lengthwise. Sew a narrow panel to each side of wide panel.

2. Layer backing, batting, and quilt top; baste.

3. Quilt as desired.

TRIMMING ALBUM CROSS BLOCKS

We like to use quick cutting and piecing methods whenever possible. Sometimes, we have avoided a particular pattern if we'd need a template or complicated measuring in order to cut the pieces. The Album Cross block, with its pointy-ended bars, was just such a pattern.

Liz invented this clever trimming method that we use for large Album Cross blocks. By using oversized rectangle and triangle pieces and then trimming the block, she made making perfectly accurate blocks a snap. The pointy ends are created in the trimming process—no template required!

To set yourself up for trimming blocks, you'll need a 9½" ruled square, a rotary cutter, freezer paper, a pencil, and tape.

1. Use rotary cutter and ruler to cut a 1⅞" square from paper to use as a centering guide when trimming blocks.

2. Using large square ruler, draw an 8½" square on a piece of paper. Draw lines to divide the square in quarters into 4 (4¼") squares.

3. Place large square ruler atop positioning guide drawing, aligning the 8½" marks on the square ruler with edges of the 8½" square you have drawn. Position 1⅞" paper square atop ruler so corners of paper square are aligned with center dividing lines on positioning guide drawing, as shown in *Photo 1*. Tape the paper square in place.

4. Referring to *Photo 2*, place prepared square ruler atop block, aligning paper square on ruler within the outline of the block center. Trim excess block along 2 adjacent sides of ruler.

5. Rotate block and reposition ruler so 8½" marks on ruler are aligned with trimmed corner and paper square is aligned with block center as shown in *Photo 3*. Trim remaining 2 sides of block. Trimmed block measures 8½" square and will finish 8" square.

Photo 1

Photo 2

Photo 3

MEMORY PHOTO WALL QUILT

Marianne chose favorite photographs of her three daughters for this special wall quilt. She used a color ink jet photocopier to print the photos directly onto fabric. You can also use an ink jet computer printer to print in this way.

Machine pieced
and quilted by
Marianne Fons

Finished size   35" x 44"
Blocks   12 (9") blocks

MATERIALS

❑ Scraps (approximately ½ yard each) of assorted yellow print fabrics and assorted blue print fabrics for blocks
❑ ½ yard of white 100% cotton "memory cloth" (200 thread-count muslin)
❑ ¼ yard of dark blue print fabric for inner border

❑ ¾ yard of yellow print fabric for outer border and binding
❑ 1½ yards of fabric for quilt back
❑ Crib-size batting
❑ 9½" or larger ruled square

CUTTING

Measurements for cutting include ¼" seam allowances. Cut all strips across fabric width.

From assorted yellow and blue scraps, cut:
- 1½"-wide, 2"-wide, and 2½" wide strips in a variety of fabrics.

From dark blue, cut:
- 4 (1½"-wide) strips. Trim 2 strips to 36½" long for inner side borders and 2 strips to 29½" long for end borders.

From yellow print, cut:
- 4 (3½"-wide) strips. Trim 2 strips to 38½" long for outer side borders and 2 strips to 35½" long for end borders.
- 4 (2¼"-wide) strips for binding.

BLOCK ASSEMBLY

1. Refer to Color Copier Quilts on pages 46-47 and make 12 (approximately 4" x 6") fabric rectangles with photos printed on them.

2. Trim edges of 1 fabric photo rectangle at odd angles. Be sure to include ¼" seam allowances beyond image area you wish to include.

3. Choose 2 blue strips of same width. Join strips to opposite sides of fabric photo. Trim edges of strips even with top and bottom edges of fabric photo.

4. Choose 2 blue strips of a different fabric. Join strips to top and bottom edges of fabric photo. Trim edges of strips even with sides of fabric photo.

5. Continue in this manner until framed photo is larger than 9½" square.

6. Position 9½" ruled square atop framed photo. Trim edges so framed photo is 9½" square.

7. Make 6 blue blocks and 6 yellow blocks.

QUILT ASSEMBLY

1. Referring to photograph on page 44, lay out blocks in 4 horizontal rows with 3 blocks in each row, alternating colors of blocks.

2. Join blocks in horizontal rows. Join rows.

3. Join 1½" x 36½" blue borders to quilt sides. Join 1½" x 29½" blue borders to top and bottom edges.

4. Join 3½" x 38½" borders to quilt sides. Join 3½" x 35½" borders to top and bottom edges.

FINISHING

1. Layer backing, batting, and quilt top; baste.

2. Quilt as desired. Quilt shown was machine quilted in-the-ditch around photo blocks and framing pieces.

COLOR COPIER QUILTS

Ink jet color copying methods developed by the Hewlett Packard company in Corvalis, Oregon, have enabled quilters to easily and inexpensively include color photo images in their quilts. Color ink jet photocopiers and computer printers now cost about the same as other home-use copiers and printers.

Any quilter can use a few simple techniques to prepare fabric for image printing. Once you've printed your favorite photos onto fabric, you can work these special fabric pieces into a memory quilt as Marianne did. You can also use these methods to create special labels for your quilts. The methods described here are applicable for color ink jet computer printers as well as inkjet color copiers.

CHOOSING PHOTOS FOR QUILTS

Marianne pored over her family photo albums to select the perfect photos for her memory quilt. She narrowed her selection down to four special pictures of each of her three daughters. Here's our advice for snapshot selection:

- Use photos that have sharp, clear focus.
- Choose simple photos in which the subject matter, whether a person, a pet, a car, or a home, is prominent.
- Avoid pictures with too much background. Close-ups are best.
- Avoid photos that have distracting extra images, such as trees or poles that seem to be growing behind a person's head!

THE COLOR COPY MACHINE

We used a Hewlett Packard 140 Color Copier for our color photo blocks. To find a dealer near you, call Hewlett Packard at 541-715-2000, or visit their web site, www.hp.com/go/copiers.

FABRICS FOR COLOR COPIER QUILTS

For best results, use fabric that is tightly woven. When color images are printed on coarsely-woven fabric, the prominent fabric texture makes the photo appear grainy. We used 200-count 100% cotton broadcloth, which is available in pure white or off-white. Check your local quilt shop for this kind of fabric, sometimes called "memory cloth," or call Fons & Porter Quilt Supply at 1-888-985-1020.

PREPARING FABRIC FOR PERMANENT COPYING

If your quilt is intended for use that will require laundering, prepare your fabric so that the copied images will be more permanent.

1. Soak fabric in Downey® Ultra Free fabric softener (or other fabric softener that has no added dyes or fragrances) mixed half and half with water. Soak for 15 minutes. Rinse under running water 20-30 seconds. Hang to dry. Iron until fabric is flat and smooth.

2. Mount your fabric on freezer paper as described below.

3. Spray with anti-static spray such as Static Guard®. Allow fabric to dry completely before copying.

4. Copy images onto prepared fabric pieces.

5. After copying, spray image area with a clear artist's fixative or varnish. Hewlett-Packard recommends Krylon® Workable Fixatif #1306, Blair® Matte Spray Fix, or Deft® Semi-Gloss Clear Wood Finish (in spray can). Be sure to test any of these first to make sure the colors don't run and that fabric does not become too stiff.

MOUNTING FABRIC FOR COPYING

Stabilize your fabric pieces for printing with a color copier by pressing fabric to freezer paper. We recommend Reynolds® brand paper, available at most grocery stores. For best results, prepare your fabric piece under non-humid conditions.

1. Using a large ruled square and a rotary cutter, cut piece of paper 9" x 11½".

2. From tightly-woven cotton fabric, cut fabric piece 8¾" x 11¼" (slightly smaller than paper piece).

3. Using a dry iron set on "cotton," press fabric rectangle to shiny side of paper rectangle. Lay fabric piece on ironing board. Position shiny side of paper against fabric. Press so that paper adheres to fabric. Turn unit over to fabric side and press again, making sure there are no bubbles or wrinkles in fabric.

4. Using ruled square and rotary cutter, trim unit to 8½" x 11" to fit through copier. If necessary, after trimming, press cut edges again to adhere firmly.

PRE-PURCHASED FABRIC SHEETS

Cannon® and June Tailor® are two companies that market treated fabric sheets for inkjet desktop printers or color copiers. Treated sheets are available in many quilt shops or computer supply companies. You may need to trim the sheets so they fit in your copier or printer tray. Remove the plastic or other backing after printing. Wash printed sheets on the gentle cycle of your machine.

INK JET PRINTING

Once you've chosen your photos and prepared your fabric units, take time to experiment with the features of the copy machine or the photo image program on your computer. Read the instruction manual so you know about the available features. For example, you can enlarge or reduce your photos. Depending on the size you print your photos, you may be able to print two or more on one sheet making optimum use of your prepared fabric.

To save ink, time, and fabric, do your experimenting in the "black" rather than "color" mode, the "fast" copy mode, and with paper, rather than prepared fabric in the paper tray.

Once you are happy with your placement and enlargement choices, place prepared fabric in the tray, and choose "color." Choose "better," rather than "best" for the copy mode. The "best" mode uses more ink and takes longer. You will be happy with the middle ground for copying on fabric.

FROM COPIER TO QUILT

Marianne trimmed her copied images to irregular rectangles and then framed them with fabric strips. Have fun dreaming up a special setting or treatment for your own fabric photos.

YO-YO PILLOW

Evalee Waltz made this yo-yo pillow simi-lar to an antique pillow that belongs to a friend. Evalee used a variety of sizes of yo-yos for the basket and flowers and bias for the flower stems. As an added touch, she used decorative buttons as the centers of some flowers.

Finished size   19" square, plus ruffle

MATERIALS

- ❏ ⅝ yard of cream solid fabric for pillow front
- ❏ 1½ yards of pink print fabric for ruffle and back
- ❏ ¼ yard of pink solid fabric for basket
- ❏ ⅛ yard of green solid fabric for stems
- ❏ Scraps of assorted pastel print fabrics for yo-yos
- ❏ Polyester fiberfill for stuffing pillow
- ❏ 2 (½"-diameter) yellow buttons for medium flower centers
- ❏ Template material or freezer paper
- ❏ Quilting thread or other strong thread

CUTTING

Make 1"-, 2"-, 3"-, and 4"-diameter circle templates from template material or freezer paper. Circle patterns are on page 49. As an alternative to making templates, you can trace around common household objects such as the top of a spool of thread, a drinking glass, or other round objects that are approximately these sizes.

From cream solid fabric, cut:
- ■ 1 (19½") square for pillow front.

From pink print fabric, cut:
- ■ 5 (6"-wide) strips for ruffle.
- ■ 1 (19½") square for pillow back.

From pink solid fabric, cut:
- ■ 61 (2"-diameter) circles for basket.

From green solid fabric, cut:
- ■ 7 (1¼" x 5") bias strips for stems. Fold strips in thirds lengthwise and press to form approximately ¼"-wide stems.

From assorted pastel prints, cut:
- ■ 10 (1"-diameter) circles for tiny yo-yos (cut 6 from 1 fabric for cluster flower and 3 from yellow and 1 from pink to use as flower centers).
- ■ 4 (2"-diameter) circles for small yo-yos.
- ■ 6 (3"-diameter) circles for medium yo-yos.
- ■ 1 (4"-diameter) circle for large yo-yo.

MAKING YO-YOS

No one knows who invented the fabric yo-yo, but we do know they have been in and out of fashion at least since the 1930s, when they were popularized in ladies' magazines. Other names for these little gathered circles of fabric are powder puffs, pucker puffs, bon bons, and rosettes. In England, they are called Suffolk puffs.

To make yo-yos, you need assorted fabric scraps, pencil, freezer paper, scissors, an iron, quilting thread, and a needle.

1. Use a household template such as a jar lid or drinking glass to mark circles for cutting, or make a template from one of the patterns below. Yo-yos will finish slightly smaller than half the diameter of your household template. For example, a circle a little larger than 4" across will make 2" yo-yos.

2. Position your template against the smooth side of freezer paper and draw around the edge with pencil. Cut out freezer paper template. You may want to make several paper templates.

3. Stack 3 or 4 fabric scraps that are larger than your paper template. Use a dry iron set at "wool" to press shiny side of paper template to top fabric piece.

4. Cut out stack of circles, cutting along edge of paper template. In this manner, cut out the number of fabric circles you need. Each freezer paper template can be reused several times.

5. Turn under raw edge of a fabric circle ¼", turning so that wrong sides are facing. Use needle and quilting thread to make running stitches, sewing all the way around the circle.

6. Pull on thread to gather circle with right side of fabric facing out. Make a final stitch and tie a knot to secure yo-yo. The gathered side is the front.

7. Make number of yo-yos needed for your project.

8. Join yo-yos by placing two units together, gathered sides facing. Using thread that blends with fabrics, whipstitch units together on one side. Join yo-yos into rows; join rows as needed to create design.

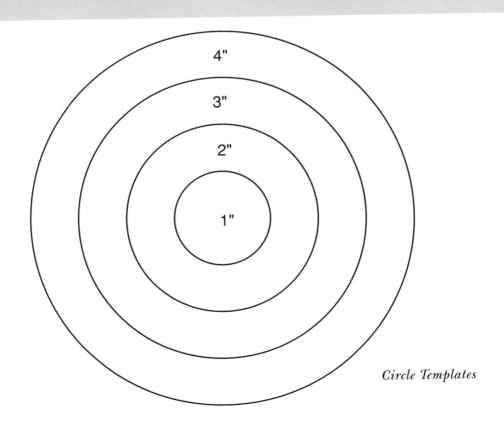

Circle Templates

PILLOW TOP ASSEMBLY

1. Join pink solid yo-yos in 1 row of 3, 2 rows of 5, 1 row of 7, 1 row of 9, and 1 row of 11 yo-yos for basket. Join 21 yo-yos into long strip for basket handle. To join yo-yos, place 2 together with front (gathered) sides facing. Using thread that blends with fabrics, whipstitch yo-yos together along one side.

2. To make basket, whipstitch rows together as shown in *Basket Diagram.* Center basket on pillow top, placing bottom of basket approximately 2" up from bottom edge. Pin basket to pillow front. Pin handle strip in place. Wait to tack basket and handle to background until all flowers and stems are stitched in place.

3. Join 1 tiny yellow yo-yo and 6 matching tiny yo-yos to make cluster flower, placing yellow yo-yo in center.

4. Referring to *Basket Diagram,* arrange bias stems, small, medium, and large yo-yos, and cluster flower. Trim stems to desired lengths, concealing raw ends of stems behind top row of basket or flowers. Appliqué stems in place.

5. Referring to photograph and *Basket Diagram,* arrange 2 small yo-yos, 6 medium yo-yos, 1 large yo-yo, and 1 cluster flower on pillow top for flowers, covering ends of stems. Pin flower yo-yos in place. Use remaining tiny yo-yos for centers of medium yo-yo flowers and remaining small yo-yo as center of large flower. Choose a yo-yo or button for center of each yo-yo flower. Place center yo-yo atop yo-yo flowers. Stitch center yo-yo or button through all layers to tack pieces in place. Stitch the center of the cluster flower to background.

6. Tack basket and handle yo-yos to background.

PILLOW FINISHING

1. Join 6"-wide pink strips together to form loop for ruffle. Fold ruffle in half with wrong sides facing so it is 3" wide; press. Divide ruffle into 4 equal sections; mark divisions with pins. Run gathering thread around ruffle loop, a scant ¼" from raw edges.

2. Draw around a mug or large glass to round off corners of pillow top. Use pins to mark centers of pillow sides. Gather ruffle so that ¼ of ruffle is distributed between each quadrant of pillow top. Aligning raw edges of ruffle with edges of pillow top and rounded corner markings, pin ruffle in place. Baste ruffle to pillow top.

3. Pin pillow top to pillow back with right sides facing. Working with wrong side of pillow top facing up so you can use basting stitching as stitching guide, stitch pillow top to pillow back, leaving approximately 8" open along 1 side to turn and stuff pillow. Hard stitch opening closed.

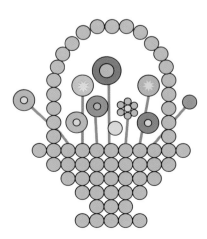

Basket Diagram

CHARACTERISTICS OF DEPRESSION-ERA QUILTS

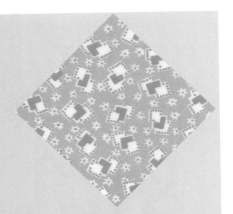

Ironically, we refer to quilts made between 1920-1940 as "Depression Quilts" when they are probably the cheeriest quilts in American quilt history! Techniques for synthetic dyeing developed after World War I made new pastel and bright colors available for fabrics.

Among the popular new colors were goldenrod yellow, buttercup yellow, baby blue, royal blue, "kitchen" green, baby pink, hot pink, coral, lavender, and peach.

Print styles during this time period included many "busy," medium to large-scale, high-contrast florals. Pictured here are a few reproductions of 1930s-style prints currently available. Quilters toned these busy fabrics down by combining them with calming solid colors. Instead of using the shirting prints popular in the nineteenth century and early twentieth, the Depression-era quilters used muslin or off-white solid fabric for the background areas of their blocks.

During these hard financial times, many homemakers used feed or flour sacks to fashion family clothing and quilts. Clever marketers came up with the idea of printed cloth for bags of staples, and quilters were delighted. People today can still remember their mother or grandmother carefully selecting matching printed bags of chicken or other livestock feed, seed, flour, or sugar in order to have enough fabric for a dress or quilt.

Though virtually every woman had access to a sewing machine, many of the patterns popular during the Depression were more suited to hand piecing. Domestic skills were praised in ladies' magazines of the times, and women prided themselves on being able to sew a perfect seam or bake the best apple pie.

Block-style patchwork and appliqué quilts were popular, often with alternate plain setting squares or sashing strips in solid color fabric. Other fashionable quilt styles were appliqué medallions and one-patch designs like Grandmother's Flower Garden.

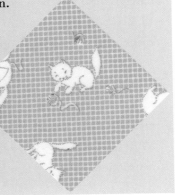

PANSY BABY QUILT

We combined innovative appliqué techniques, such as fusible web and machine blanket stitching, to create this charming crib-size quilt made from 1930s reproduction fabrics. Blanket stitching with black thread around appliqué pieces was a popular appliqué method during the Depression Era. The green and white checkerboard and lattice sashing make this quilt special. Lavender, medium blue, yellow, and pink were other popular solid colors during this time period that would also work well for the sashing.

Finished size   36" x 47"
Blocks   12 (8") blocks

MATERIALS

❑ 48 (3½") squares of assorted print fabrics for flower petals
❑ ⅜ yard of green solid fabric for leaves
❑ ⅛ yard of yellow solid fabric for flower centers
❑ 1½ yards of white or off-white solid fabric for block backgrounds and sashing
❑ 1¼ yards of green solid fabric for sashing and binding
❑ 1½ yards of fabric for quilt back
❑ Crib-size batting
❑ 8" square of freezer paper, folded diagonally in both directions
❑ *Optional:* Paper-backed fusible web
❑ Black sewing thread for machine stitching or black embroidery floss and hand sewing needle

CUTTING

Measurements include ¼" seam allowances. Cut crosswise strips. Make templates for patterns on page 55. If using fusible web, follow manufacturer's instructions.

From each assorted print fabric square, cut:
■ 1 flower petal (48 total).

From green solid fabric, cut:
■ 48 leaves.

From yellow solid fabric, cut:
■ 12 flower centers.

From white solid fabric, cut:
■ 3 (8½"-wide) strips. From these, cut 12 (8½") squares for block backgrounds.
■ 12 (1½"-wide) strips for strip sets.

From green solid fabric, cut:
■ 18 (1½"-wide) strips for strip sets.
■ 5 (2¼"-wide) strips for binding.

BLOCK ASSEMBLY

1. Trace positioning guide on page 55 onto 8" paper square. Darken lines.
2. Lightly press background square diagonally both ways. Lay square atop positioning guide.
3. Referring to *Block Diagram,* arrange 4 leaves, 4 flower petals, and 1 flower center on background.

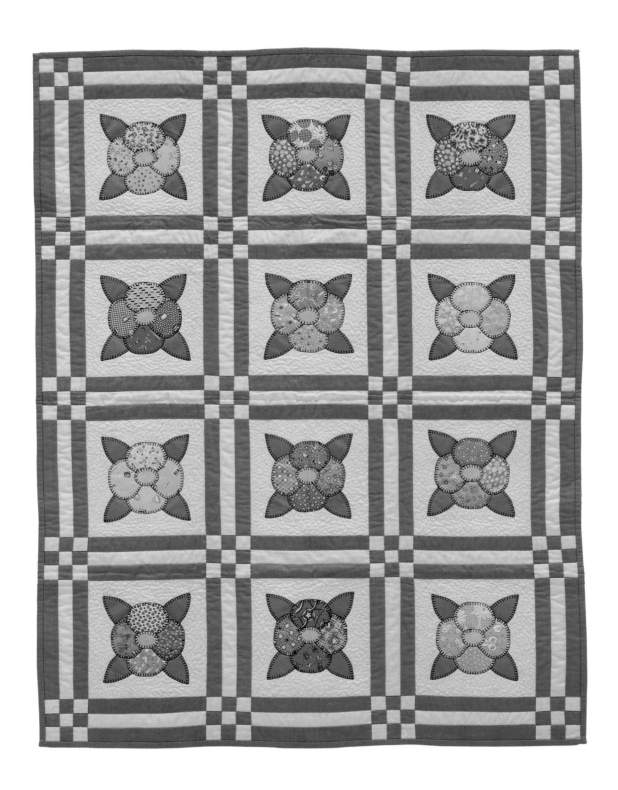

Designed by   Liz Porter

Machine appliquéd by   Marty Freed

Machine quilted by   Lynn Witzenburg

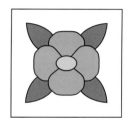

Block Diagram

4. Appliqué pieces to background square. We fused our pieces and then stitched around them with machine blanket stitching, using black thread. If you desire, use 2 strands of embroidery floss and hand blanket stitch around pieces. (See Blanket Stitch Appliqué, bottom right.)

5. Make 12 Pansy blocks.

QUILT ASSEMBLY

1. Join 1 green solid fabric strip to each side of 1 white solid fabric strip as shown in *Strip Set A Diagram.* Press seam allowances toward dark strips. Repeat to make a total of 8 strip sets.

   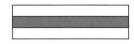

Strip Set A Diagram   *Strip Set B Diagram*

2. From each A strip set, cut 4 (8½"-wide) segments for sashing strips and 3 (1½"-wide) segments for nine patch sashing squares.

3. Join 1 white solid fabric strip to each side of 1 green solid fabric strip as shown in *Strip Set B Diagram.* Press seam allowances toward dark strip. Repeat to make a total of 2 strip sets.

4. From B strip sets, cut a total of 40 (1½"-wide) segments for nine patch sashing squares.

5. Join 1½"-wide segments as shown in *Nine Patch Diagrams.* Make 20 nine patch sashing squares.

Nine Patch Diagrams

6. Referring to Pre-Sashing Blocks for Quicker Setting on page 57, assemble the quilt top.

FINISHING

1. Mark quilting designs as desired. Quilt shown was machine quilted in-the-ditch along sashing strips and squares. Flower shapes were outline quilted with meander quilting in block backgrounds.

2. Layer quilt back, batting, and quilt top; baste.

3. Quilt as desired.

BLANKET-STITCH APPLIQUÉ

For hand stitching, use two or three strands of cotton embroidery floss, or a single strand of size 8 pearl cotton. Follow the diagram below to secure your appliqués in place with hand stitching.

If your sewing machine does a blanket stitch, begin by experimenting with stitch length and width settings. Make some samples to practice on by fusing some of your fabric scraps to pieces of the background fabric you are using in your quilt. Use regular cotton sewing thread on the top and in the bobbin. Secure ends of stitching by pulling threads to the back and tying them off. If your background fabric is light weight, you may need to position a piece of paper stabilizer underneath your block before you stitch to prevent tunneling. Tear the paper away once stitching is complete.

Blanket Stitch Diagram

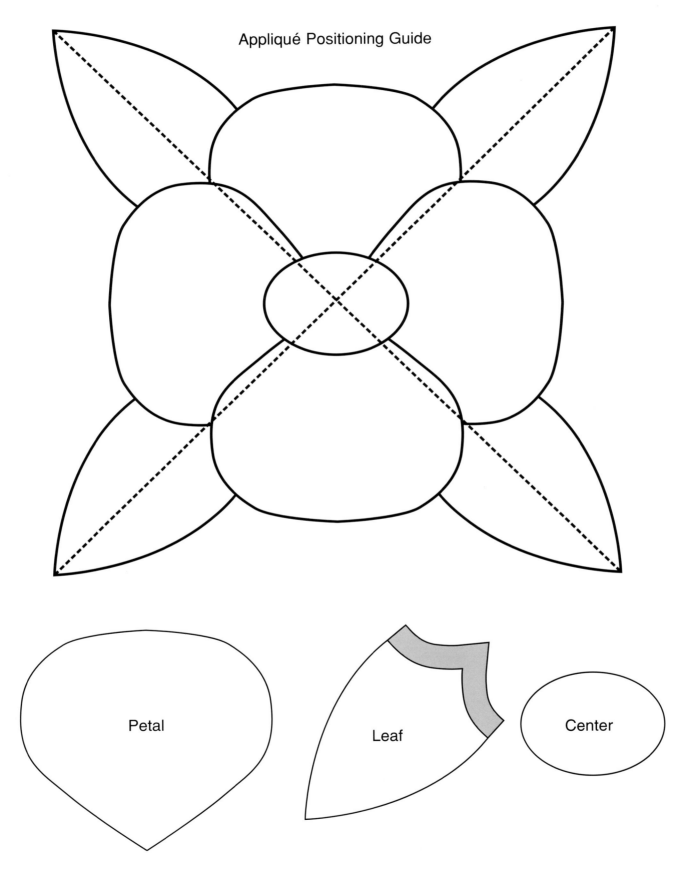

Appliqué Positioning Guide

Petal

Leaf

Center

"Windowing" is a nifty way to eliminate the stiffness of fused appliqués. Quilt shops and fabric stores carry several brands of paper backed fusible web. Choose a lightweight, "sewable" fusible product; two of our favorite brands are Aleene's Fusible Web® and Wonder Under®. Always read and follow the manufacturer's instructions for proper fusing time and iron temperature.

Here are the basic steps for our "windowing" method:

1. Use a pencil to trace appliqué motifs onto the paper side of the fusible web, making a separate tracing for each appliqué you need as shown in *Diagram 1*.

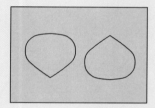

Diagram 1

2. Cut out drawn appliqué shapes, cutting them a bit larger than drawn lines as shown in *Diagram 2*.

Diagram 2

3. To "window" the fusible web, trim web from the interior of the appliqué shape, leaving a scant ¼" to the inside of the drawn outline as shown in *Diagram 3*.

Diagram 3

4. Follow manufacturer's instructions to fuse the web side of each shape to the wrong side of the appliqué fabric as shown in *Diagram 4*.

Diagram 4

5. Cut out appliqués, cutting carefully on drawn outline as shown in *Diagram 5*. Only a thin band of fusible web frames the shape.

Diagram 5

6. Peel off paper backing, position appliqué in place on background fabric, and follow manufacturer's instructions to fuse shapes in place. Fuse shapes, working from the background to the foreground for designs with overlapping pieces.
7. Machine or hand blanket stitch the appliqué shapes to the background.

When you make a quilt that has sashing and corner squares between the rows of blocks, you are usually instructed to construct two types of rows—block rows and sashing rows. The block rows are made up of blocks alternating with sashing strips, and the sashing rows are made up of sashing strips alternating with sashing squares. Once you get these rows assembled, you join them with long horizontal or vertical seams.

Our method of "pre-sashing" means you add sashing and sashing squares to the blocks ahead of time. It lets you avoid dealing with those long skinny rows of sashing and squares. We used pre-sashing techniques for the Pansy, Flower Pot, Partridge Garden Maze, and several other quilts in this book.

1. Sew a sashing strip to the left side of a block as shown in *Diagram 1*. Press seam allowances toward the sashing strip. Repeat for all blocks.

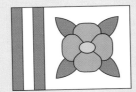

Diagram 1

2. Join 1 sashing square to 1 sashing strip as shown in *Diagram 2*. Press seam allowances toward the sashing strip. Repeat for all sashing squares and sashing strips. You will have 1 extra sashing square.

Diagram 2

3. Sew the sashing square/sashing strip unit to the top of the block as shown in *Diagram 3*. Repeat for all blocks.

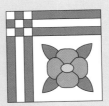

Diagram 3

4. Lay out pre-sashed blocks. To complete each row, sew a sashing square/sashing strip unit to the block at the right end of each row as shown in *Quilt Assembly Diagram*. Join rows.

5. Join sashing square/sashing strip units and single sashing square to make a sashing row for the bottom edge of the quilt. Join row to bottom edge of quilt.

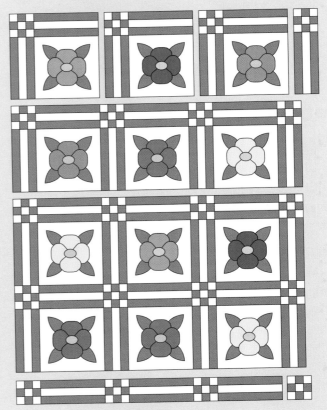

Quilt Assembly Diagram

Prosperity Wheel Quilt

When Marianne visited a quilt guild in Guyman, Oklahoma, one of the members brought an antique quilt top in a variation of this pattern for show and tell. Inspired by the antique version, Marianne created her own Prosperity Wheel quilt from 1930s-style reproduction fabrics.

Finished size   89½" x 109⅜"
Blocks   32 (12") blocks

Materials

❑ 36 fat quarters* of assorted pastel print fabrics for spokes and prairie points
❑ 3¼ yards of yellow solid fabric for hubs, sashing squares, and borders
❑ 7 yards of cream solid fabric for block backgrounds, setting triangles, and sashing strips
❑ 9 yards of fabric for quilt back
❑ Queen-size quilt batting
❑ Freezer paper for templates
Fat quarter = 18" x 22"

Cutting

Measurements include ¼" seam allowances. Patterns for Spoke, Hub, and Background Cut-Away are on page 62. Trace 12 Spoke patterns, 4 Hub patterns, and 4 Background Cut-Away patterns onto freezer paper. Cut out templates. To use freezer paper templates, use hot, dry iron to press shiny side of paper onto fabric. Cut around edge of templates. Replace paper templates when they no longer adhere to fabric or as needed. Special instructions for using the Background Cut-Away pattern to trim background squares and side setting triangles are on page 60.

From each pastel print fabric, cut:
■ 12 Spoke pieces (You will have 6 extra.)
■ 4 (3½") squares for prairie points (You will have 2 extra.)

From yellow solid fabric, cut:
■ 3 (2½") wide strips. From these, cut 49 (2½") sashing squares.
■ 1 (100"-long) piece cut lengthwise from fabric. From this, cut:
   ■ 2 (5½" x 99⅞") side borders.
   ■ 2 (5½" x 90") end borders.
   ■ 142 Hub pieces.

From cream solid fabric, cut:
■ 2 (18¼"-wide) strips. From these, cut 4 (18¼") squares. Cut each square in quarters diagonally to make 16 quarter-square side setting triangles. You will have 2 extra.

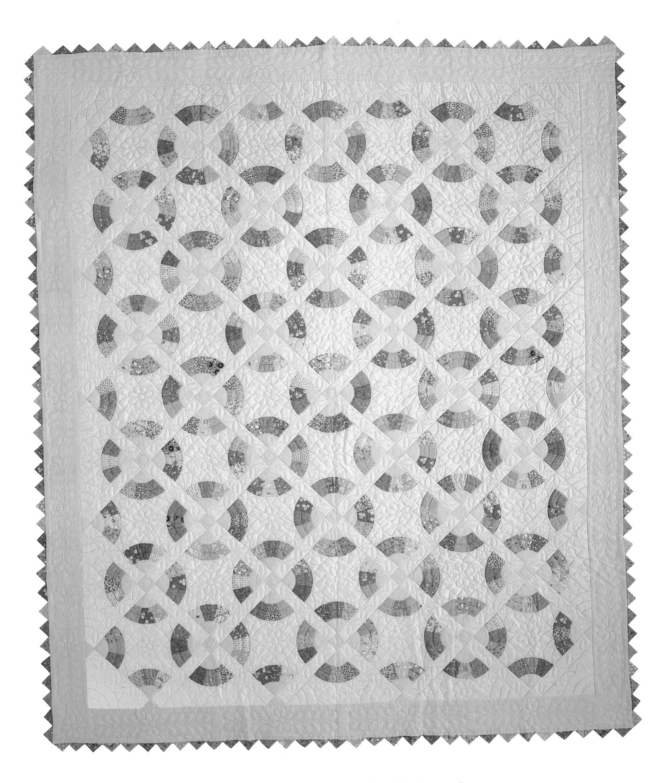

Designed and machine pieced by   Marianne Fons

Hand quilted by   Ada Troyer, Verna Troyer

Katie Troyer and Mary Yoder

■ 1 (9⅜"-wide) strip. From this cut, 2 (9⅜") squares. Cut each square in half diagonally to make 4 half-square corner setting triangles.
■ 5 (12½"-wide) strips. From these, cut 80 (2½" x 12½") rectangles for sashing strips.
■ 11 (12½"-wide) strips. From these, cut 32 (12½") background squares.

BACKGROUND SQUARES AND SIDE SETTING TRIANGLES PREPARATION

1. Align and press 1 Background Cut-Away template at each corner of 1 background square as shown in *Template Positioning Diagram*. Place 3 background squares beneath square with templates; pin layers.

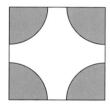 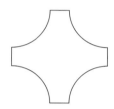

Template Positioning Diagram   *Background Piece Diagram*

2. Cut around Background Cut-Away templates, removing pie-shaped piece from each corner of background squares as shown in *Background Piece Diagram*. In this manner, trim all background squares.

3. Align and press 1 Background Cut-Away template to right-angle corner of 1 side setting triangle as shown in *Template Positioning Diagram*. Place 3 side setting triangles beneath triangle with template; pin layers. Cut around Background Cut-Away template, removing pie-shaped piece from corner of

Template Positioning Diagram   *Side Setting Triangle Diagram*

triangle. In this manner, trim all side setting triangles. Do not trim corner setting triangles.

SPOKE AND HUB ASSEMBLY

1. Join 3 Spoke pieces as shown in *Spoke Assembly Diagram*. Fold assembled Spoke pieces in half to find center of outer and inner curves. Mark center points with pins or by pressing or clipping.

Spoke Assembly Diagram   *Spoke/Hub Diagram*

2. Fold 1 Hub in half to find center of curve. Mark center point with pin or by pressing or clipping.
3. Working with Spoke unit on top, pin Hub to Spoke unit. Align centers of curves and ends of pieces. Join Hub to Spoke unit.
4. Make 142 Spoke/Hub units as shown in *Spoke/Hub Diagram*.

BLOCK AND SIDE SETTING TRIANGLE ASSEMBLY

1. Fold 1 curved section of 1 background piece in half to determine center of curve. Mark center point on curve with pin or by pressing or clipping.
2. Working with background piece on top, pin Spoke/Hub unit to curve on background piece. Align centers of curves and ends of pieces. Join

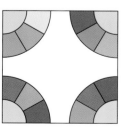 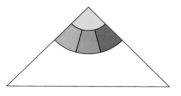

Block Diagram   *Side Setting Triangle Diagram*

Spoke/Hub unit to background piece. Repeat to join Spoke/Hub units to remaining 3 curves as shown in *Block Diagram.*

3. Make 32 Prosperity Wheel blocks.

4. In a similar manner, join Spoke/Hub unit to all side setting triangles as shown in *Side Setting Triangle Diagram.*

PRAIRIE POINT ASSEMBLY

1. Choose 142 (3½") print squares for prairie points.

2. Fold 1 square in half diagonally with wrong sides facing to form triangle. Fold in half diagonally again to form smaller triangle as shown in *Prairie Point Diagrams.*

Prairie Point Diagrams

QUILT ASSEMBLY

1. Referring to *Quilt Assembly Diagram,* lay out blocks, sashing strips, sashing squares, side setting triangles, and corner triangles.

2. Join pieces in diagonal rows. Join rows.

3. Trim excess sashing squares even with edges of setting triangles.

4. Join 5½" x 99⅞" borders to opposite sides of quilt top. Join 5½" x 90" borders to top and bottom edges.

5. Aligning raw edges of prairie point triangles with raw edge of right side of border, evenly distribute 32 prairie points along top edge of quilt. Tuck ends of prairie points inside each other along quilt edge as shown in *Adding Prairie Points Diagram.* Pin prairie points in place. Machine baste prairie points to border. Repeat for bottom border.

6. In a similar manner, join 39 prairie points to each side border.

Adding Prairie Points Diagram

Quilt Assembly Diagram

FINISHING

1. Mark quilting designs as desired.

2. Divide backing fabric into 3 (3-yard) panels. Join 3 panels. Seams on quilt back will run parallel to top edge of quilt.

3. Layer quilt back, batting, and quilt top; baste.

4. Quilt as desired. Leave outer 1" of borders unquilted to facilitate finishing prairie points. Arc quilting design and flower quilting design for blocks and setting triangles are on page 63. A leaf pattern was quilted in sashing strips, a circle in sashing squares, and a feather design combined with the flower quilting design in borders.

5. Trim backing and batting even with raw edge of quilt top. Trim away an additional ¼" of batting.

6. Turn prairie points so they face out from quilt top, bringing raw edge of quilt top to inside. Turn in ¼" of quilt back. Blindstitch folded edge of backing to seam line on back side of prairie points.

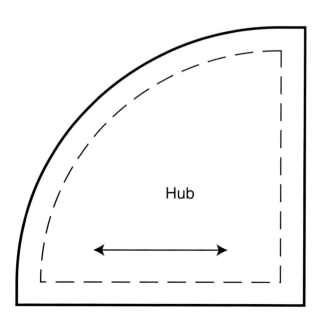

Hub

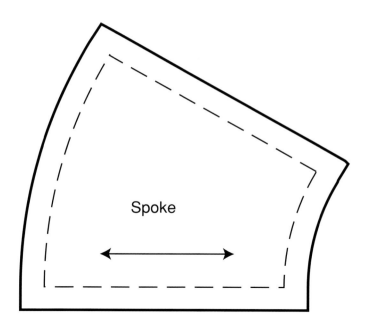

Spoke

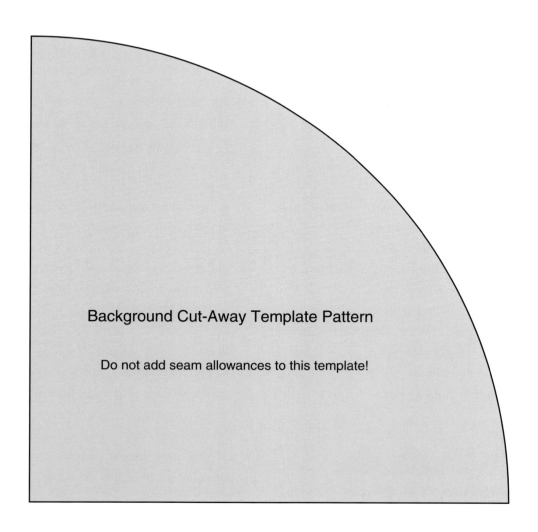

Background Cut-Away Template Pattern

Do not add seam allowances to this template!

Flower Quilting Design

Arc Quilting Design

PROSPERITY WHEEL WALL QUILT

We worked with this Amish version of Prosperity Wheel on our television show episode and liked it so much we finished it up after filming was completed. We love how the vivid solid colors sparkle on the black background.

Made by

Shoney Jones

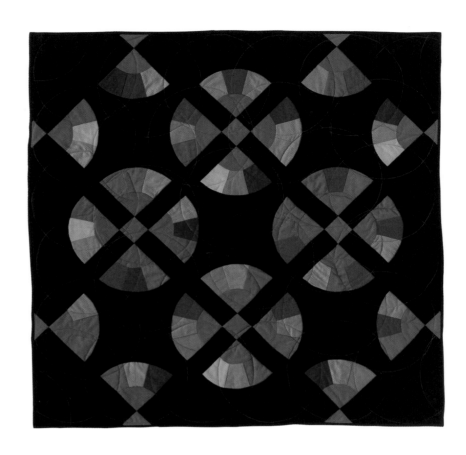

Finished size   39½" x 39½"
Blocks   5 (12") blocks

MATERIALS

❏ 12 fat eighths* of assorted jewel tone solid fabrics for spokes
❏ ¼ yard of fuchsia solid fabric for hubs and sashing squares
❏ 2¼ yards of black solid fabric for block backgrounds, setting triangles, and sashing strips
❏ 1¼ yards of fabric for quilt back
❏ 45" x 45" piece of quilt batting
❏ Freezer paper for templates
Fat eighth = 9" x 22"

CUTTING

Measurements include ¼" seam allowances.
Patterns for Spoke, Hub, and Background Cut-

Away are on page 62. Trace 6 Spoke patterns, 4 Hub patterns, and 4 Background Cut-Away patterns onto freezer paper. Cut out templates. To use freezer paper templates, use hot, dry iron to press shiny side of paper onto fabric. Cut around edge of templates. Replace paper templates when they no longer adhere to fabric or as needed. Special instructions for using the Background Cut-Away pattern to trim background squares and side setting triangles are on page 65.

From each jewel tone solid fabric, cut:
■ 6 Spokes.

From fuchsia solid fabric, cut:
■ 1 (2½"-wide) strip. From this, cut 12 (2½") sashing squares.
■ 24 Hubs.

From black solid fabric, cut:

- 2 (12½"-wide) strips. From these, cut 5 (12½") background squares.
- 6 (2½"-wide) strips. From these, cut 16 (2½" x 12½") rectangles for sashing strips.
- 4 (2¼"-wide) strips for binding.
- 1 (18¼") square. Cut square in quarters diagonally to make 4 quarter-square side setting triangles.
- 2 (9⅜") squares. Cut each square in half diagonally to make 4 half-square corner setting triangles.

BACKGROUND SQUARES AND SIDE SETTING TRIANGLES PREPARATION

1. Referring to *Template Positioning Diagram,* align and press 1 Background Cut-Away template at each corner of 1 background square. Place 4 background squares beneath square with templates and pin layers.

2. Cut around Background Cut-Away templates, removing pie-shaped piece from each corner of background squares as shown in *Background Piece Diagram.*

Template Positioning Diagram   *Background Piece Diagram*

3. To trim setting triangles, align and press 1 Background Cut-Away template to right-angle corner of 1 side setting triangle as shown in *Template Positioning Diagram* for setting triangles. Place remaining 3 side setting triangles beneath triangle with template; pin layers.

4. Cut around Background Cut-Away template, removing pie-shaped piece from corner of triangles as shown in *Setting Triangle Diagram.* Do not trim corner setting triangles.

Template Positioning Diagram   *Setting Triangle Diagram*

SPOKE AND HUB ASSEMBLY

1. Join 3 Spoke pieces as shown in *Spoke Assembly Diagram.* Fold assembled Spoke pieces in half to find center of outer and inner curves. Mark center points with pins or by pressing or clipping. (See Conquering Curve-A-Phobia on page 66.)

Spoke Assembly Diagram

2. Fold 1 Hub in half to find center of curve. Mark center point with pin or by pressing or clipping.

3. Working with Spoke unit on top, pin Hub to Spoke unit. Align centers of curves and ends of pieces. Join Hub to Spoke unit.

4. Make 24 Spoke/Hub units as shown in *Spoke/Hub Diagram.*

Spoke/Hub Diagram

BLOCK AND SIDE SETTING TRIANGLE ASSEMBLY

1. Fold 1 curved section of 1 background piece in half to determine center of curve. Mark center point on curve with pin or by pressing or clipping.

2. Working with background piece on top, pin Spoke/Hub unit to curve on background piece. Align centers of curves and ends of pieces. Join Spoke/Hub unit to background piece. Repeat to join Spoke/Hub units to remaining 3 curves as shown in *Block Diagram.*

3. Make 5 Prosperity Wheel blocks.

Side Setting Triangle Diagram

Block Diagram

4. In a similar manner, join 1 Spoke/Hub unit to each side setting triangle as shown in *Side Setting Triangle Diagram.*

QUILT ASSEMBLY

1. Referring to *Quilt Assembly Diagram,* lay out blocks, sashing strips, sashing squares, side setting triangles, and corner triangles.

2. Join pieces in diagonal rows. Join rows. Trim excess sashing squares even with edges of quilt top.

FINISHING

1. Mark quilting designs as desired. Quilt shown was machine quilted with randomly spaced 10"-diameter circles. *Note: A dinner plate makes a handy circle template to mark these quilting lines.*

2. Layer quilt back, batting, and quilt top; baste.

3. Quilt as desired.

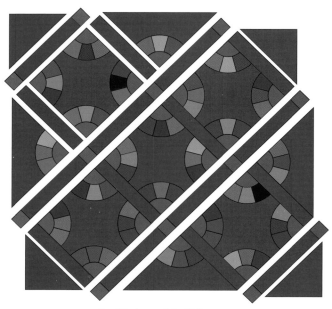

Quilt Assembly Diagram

CONQUERING CURVE-A-PHOBIA

Don't be afraid of machine stitching curved seams! We like to think of the quarter-circle piece as the "pie," and the other piece as the "crust." Follow these steps for successful curved seam piecing:

1. Fold "pie" unit in half and finger press the middle of the curved edge.

2. Fold the "crust" unit in half and finger press.

3. Place the two units right sides together with the "pie" on the bottom and the "crust" on the top. Take a tiny bite with the pin as you pin at the center and a deep bite as you pin at the ends. For small units, three pins are all you need.

4. Stitch with the **"pie" on the bottom and the "crust" on top.** As you stitch, stop periodically with the needle down. Raise your presser foot and nudge fabrics so edges stay even. Try using your seam ripper or a pin to nudge fabrics.

5. Press gently to avoid stretching. On tight curves, you may need to clip seam allowances to relax the seam before pressing.

FLOWER POT WALL QUILT

Shoney Jones updated the Flower Pot pattern by choosing bright, contemporary fabrics for her cheerful wall quilt.

Made by
Shoney Jones

Finished size   16½" x 45½"
Blocks   3 (12½") blocks

MATERIALS
- ❏ ½ yard of yellow fabric for blocks
- ❏ ¾ yard of blue and black check fabric for sashing strips, border, and binding
- ❏ Fat eighth* each of purple polka dot, red print, blue print, and swirl print fabrics for flower pots, flowers, and flower centers
- ❏ Fat quarter** of green print fabric for stems and leaves
- ❏ 1 yard of fabric for quilt back
- ❏ 18" x 48" piece of quilt batting
- ❏ Template material
- ❏ Black embroidery floss and needle

Fat eighth = 9" x 22"
**Fat quarter = 18" x 22"*

CUTTING
Measurements include ¼" seam allowances. Make templates for Flower Pot, Flower Center, Leaf, Short Stem, and Long Stem patterns on page 69. Patterns are finished size; add 3⁄16" for seam allowances as you cut appliqué fabric pieces. (See Thin Metal Templates for Crisp Appliqué Edges on page 74.)

From yellow fabric, cut:
- 1 (13"-wide) strip. From this, cut 3 (13") background squares.

From blue and black check fabric, cut:
- 4 (2½"-wide) strips. From these, cut 2 (2½" x 13") sashing strips, 2 (2½" x 42") side borders, and 2 (2½" x 17") end borders.
- 4 (2¼"-wide) strips for binding.

From purple polka dot fabric, cut:
- 3 Flower Pots.

From red print and blue print fabrics, cut:
- 3 Flowers from each fabric.

From swirl print fabric, cut:
- 6 Flower Centers.

From green print fabric, cut:
- 3 Long Stems.
- 3 Short Stems.
- 24 Leaves.

BLOCK ASSEMBLY

1. Referring to photograph on page 67 and *Block Diagram,* position 8 Leaves, 1 Short Stem, 1 Long Stem, 2 Flowers, and 1 Flower Pot on background square. Appliqué pieces in order listed. Trim background from behind flowers and flower pot, leaving a scant ¼" seam allowance. Appliqué 1 Flower Center on each flower.
2. Using 3 strands of embroidery floss, make 5 French knots in center of each Flower Center.
3. Make 3 Flower Pot blocks.

Block Diagram

QUILT ASSEMBLY

1. Referring to *Quilt Assembly Diagram,* join 3 blocks and 2 (2½" x 13") sashing strips.
2. Join side borders to opposite sides of quilt top. Join end borders to top and bottom edges.

Quilt Assembly Diagram

FINISHING

1. From backing fabric, cut 2 (18"-wide) strips. From 1 strip, cut 1 (8" x 18") rectangle. Join rectangle to full-width piece to make quilt back.
2. Layer quilt back, batting, and quilt top; baste.
3. Quilt as desired. Quilt shown was machine quilted in-the-ditch around all appliqué pieces and then echo quilted around appliqué shapes at ½" intervals.

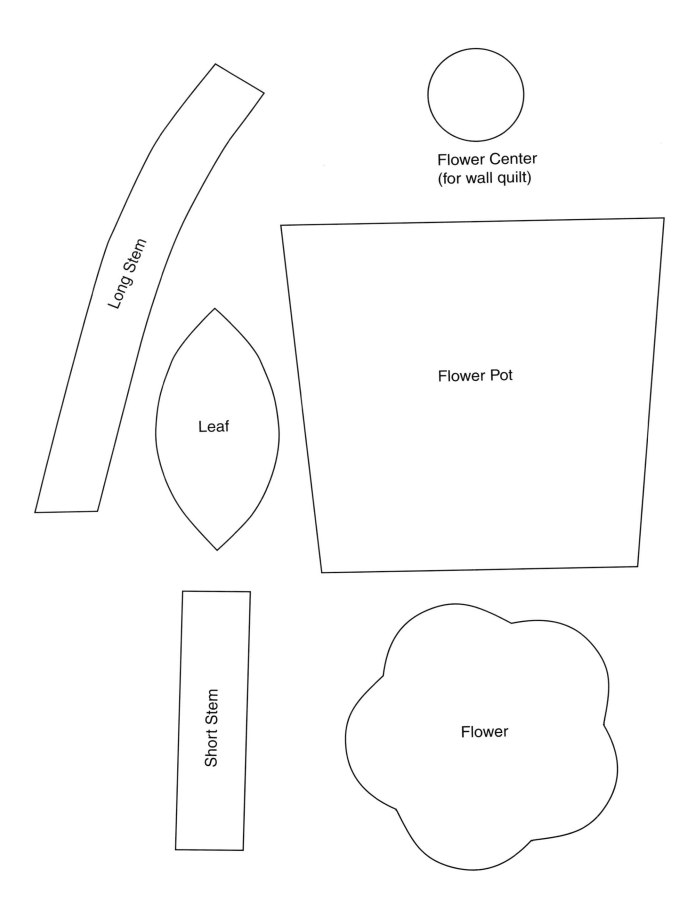

Long Stem

Flower Center
(for wall quilt)

Flower Pot

Leaf

Short Stem

Flower

FLOWER POT QUILT

Marty Freed purchased 20 appliqué Flower Pot blocks at an estate auction. The appliqué pieces were machine top stitched in place by the maker, who added black hand-stitched French knots for the flower centers. The Garden Maze set Marty, Liz, and Marianne designed is a perfect setting to show off these blocks and make a bed-sized quilt.

Finished size   75" x 92½"
Blocks   20 (12½") blocks

MATERIALS

❑ 5 yards of white solid fabric for blocks and sashing
❑ 3 yards of pink print fabric for sashing strips, sashing squares, and binding
❑ 1½ yards of green solid fabric for leaves, stems, and flower pot
❑ ¾ yard of pink solid fabric for flowers
❑ 6 yards of fabric for quilt back
❑ Double-size quilt batting
❑ Template material
❑ Black embroidery floss and needle

CUTTING

Measurements include ¼" seam allowances. Make templates for Flower Pot, Leaf, Short Stem, and Long Stem patterns on page 69 Patterns are finished size; add ³⁄₁₆" for seam allowances as you cut appliqué fabric pieces. (See Thin Metal Templates for Crisp Appliqué Edges on page 74.) Pieces for the garden maze sashing squares are cut oversized and trimmed after units are assembled.

From white solid fabric, cut:
■ 7 (13"-wide) strips. From these, cut 20 (13") background squares.
■ 17 (3½"-wide) strips for strip sets.
■ 4 (4¾"-wide) strips. From these, cut 30 (4¾") squares. Cut each square in quarters diagonally to make a total of 120 sashing square triangles.

From pink print fabric, cut:
■ 34 (1½"-wide) strips for strip sets.
■ 14 (1⅞"-wide) strips. From these, cut 30 (1⅞" x 8½") rectangles for center bars and 60 (1⅞" x 4") rectangles for short bars for sashing squares.
■ 9 (2¼"-wide) strips for binding.

From green solid fabric, cut:
■ 20 Flower Pots.
■ 160 Leaves.
■ 20 Long Stems.
■ 20 Short Stems.

From pink solid fabric, cut:
■ 40 Flowers.

Setting designed by Marty Freed, Liz Porter
and Marianne Fons

Machine quilted by Lynn Witzenburg

BLOCK ASSEMBLY

1. Referring to photo on page 71 and *Block Diagram,* position 8 Leaves, 1 Short Stem, 1 Long Stem, 2 Flowers, and 1 Flower Pot on background square. Appliqué pieces in order listed. Trim background from behind flowers and pot, leaving a scant ¼" seam allowance.

Block Assembly Diagram

2. Using 3 strands of embroidery floss, make a French knot at center of 1 flower. Surround center French knot with circle of 9 French knots. Repeat for second flower.

3. Make 20 Flower Pot blocks.

SASHING STRIP AND SQUARE ASSEMBLY

1. Join 1 (1½"-wide) pink strip to both sides of 1 (3½"-wide) white strip to make a strip set as shown in *Strip Set Diagram.* Press seam allowances toward pink strips. Make 17 strip sets.

Strip Set Diagram

2. From strip sets, cut 49 (13"-long) segments for sashing strips.

3. Referring to *Sashing Square Assembly Diagrams,* join white triangles to sides of short cross bar strips. Press seam allowances toward cross bars. Center and sew short cross bar units to both sides of long center bar. *Note: Be careful not to stretch bias edges of white triangles when sewing and pressing!*

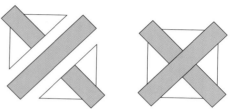

Sashing Square Assembly Diagrams

4. Position 2¾" mark on ruler atop center points of two opposite white triangles as shown in *Sashing Square Trimming Diagrams.* Trim excess fabric along edge of block. Rotate unit 180 degrees, reposition ruler, and trim. Block should now be 5½" wide.

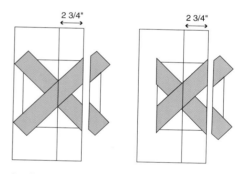

Sashing Square Trimming Diagrams

5. Repeat for remaining 2 sides so sashing square is 5½" square as shown in *Sashing Square Diagram.* Repeat to make 30 sashing squares.

Sashing Square Diagram

QUILT ASSEMBLY

1. Referring to *Quilt Assembly Diagram,* lay out blocks, sashing strips, and sashing squares. Join 5 sashing squares and 4 sashing strips to make sashing row. Make 6 sashing rows. Press seam allowances toward sashing strips. (See Pre-Sashing Blocks for Quicker Setting on page 57 for an alternative method to set this quilt.)

2. Join 4 blocks and 5 sashing strips to make block row. Make 5 block rows.

3. Join sashing rows and block rows, alternating types.

FINISHING

1. Mark quilting designs as desired.

2. Divide backing fabric into 2 (3-yard) pieces. Split 1 piece in half lengthwise. Join half panels to sides of wide panel. Press seam allowances away from center panel.

3. Layer quilt back, batting, and quilt top; baste.

4. Quilt as desired. Quilt shown was machine quilted in the ditch around all pink print strips and around appliqué pieces. A feathered quilting design was quilted in white sashing strips and on flower pot. Background squares were quilted with a diagonal grid of 1" squares.

Quilt Assembly Diagram

Thin Metal Pressing Templates for Crisp Appliqué Edges

Appliqué enthusiasts love to find quicker (no baste) ways to prepare appliqués for stitching–especially if the quick method produces crisp, sharp folds for appliqué edges. A method we've discovered recently calls for thin aluminum pressing templates–cut from disposable heavy aluminum foil pizza pans, cookie sheets, or oven liner trays you buy at the grocery store. To try this method, you'll need an aluminum pan, ball point pen, craft scissors, freezer paper, and spray starch.

1. From selected fabrics, cut out appliqués for your design, adding ³⁄₁₆" seam allowance. We recommend making finished-size freezer paper templates. Press shiny side of template to right side of fabric. Layer several pieces under top piece and cut more than one appliqué at a time.

2. To make pressing templates, place pattern atop aluminum material. Use ball point pen to trace along outlines of appliqué shapes. Press hard enough to indent the aluminum beneath the pattern.

3. Use craft scissors to cut out aluminum shapes. Cut carefully so there are no jagged edges.

4. At ironing board, position appliqué shape with wrong side facing you. Spray with starch.

5. Place metal template atop fabric shape, centering it so seam allowance extends all the way around. Use tip of iron to press the seam allowance over template. Press all the way around.

6. Remove metal template and turn appliqué right side up. Press again if necessary.

Straight-Stitch Machine Appliqué

Most quilters think of machine appliqué for quilts as a new technique. However, many appliqué quilts stitched in the 1930s, and earlier, were done by straight stitching around the appliqué shapes on a sewing machine–probably a treadle machine!

There is nothing mysterious or complicated about this technique. For best results, use an open-toe appliqué presser foot or edge-stitch foot on your machine for good visibility while stitching. If you can set your machine so that the needle stops in the down position, engage that feature before you start stitching.

1. Prepare your appliqués using your favorite method.

2. Pin appliqués in place on block background. If necessary, make a master pattern so that pieces can be placed uniformly from block to block. If some appliqué pieces overlap, work from background to foreground.

3. Using thread that matches appliqué pieces, stitch appliqués in place with a straight stitch, stitching very close to folded edge. As needed, stop stitching with needle down in fabric, lift presser foot, and pivot work before continuing.

4. Bring threads to wrong side of block and tie or secure with backstitching.

PARTRIDGE GARDEN MAZE QUILT

For her Partridge Garden Maze quilt, Liz cut 9½" blocks from partridge fabric, a print from our Savannah line of fabric for Benartex.® Our instructions are written to work with center squares this size. If you want to use this setting for blocks of a different size, keep the sashing strips the same width and adjust the length to match your block size.

Designed and pieced by   Liz Porter
Machine quilted by   Kelly Ashton

Finished size   56" x 82"
Blocks   24 (9") blocks

MATERIALS

❏ 2½ yards of blue and cream partridge print fabric
❏ 1⅝ yards of cream print fabric for centers of sashing strips and for sashing squares
❏ 2½ yards of blue print fabric for edges of sashing strips, cross bars in sashing squares, and binding
❏ 3½ yards of fabric for quilt back
❏ *Optional:* 9½" square ruler
❏ Twin-size quilt batting

CUTTING

Measurements include ¼" seam allowances. Cut crosswise strips.

From bird print or other feature fabric, cut:
■ 24 (9½") squares for blocks, centering bird pairs in each square. Cut 12 with large bird facing left and 12 with large bird facing right. (The 9½" square ruler enables you to accurately position the design motif in the center of the block.)

From cream print fabric, cut:
- 15 (2½"-wide) strips for strip sets.
- 4 (4"-wide) strips. From these, cut 35 (4") squares. Cut each square in quarters diagonally to make quarter-square triangles (140 total).

From blue print, cut:
- 30 (1½"-wide) strips for strip sets.
- 5 (1⅞"-wide) strips. From these, cut 70 (1⅞" x 3") rectangles for short cross bars in sashing squares.
- 6 (1⅞"-wide) strips. From these, cut 35 (1⅞" x 6½") rectangles for long cross bars in sashing squares.
- 8 (2¼"-wide) strips for binding.

SASHING STRIP AND SQUARE ASSEMBLY

1. Referring to *Strip Set Diagram*, join 1 (1½"-wide) blue strip to each long side of 1 cream strip. Press seam allowances toward blue strips. Make 15 strip sets.

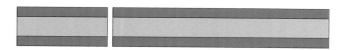

Strip Set Diagram

2. From strip sets, cut 58 (9½"-long) sashing strips.
3. Referring to *Sashing Square Assembly Diagrams*, join cream triangles to sides of short cross bar strips. Press seam allowances toward cross bars. Center and sew short cross bar units to each long side of 6½"-long center bar.

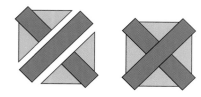

Sashing Square Assembly Diagrams

4. Referring to *Sashing Square Trimming Diagrams*, position 2¼" mark on ruler atop center points of two opposite cream triangles. Trim excess fabric along edge of block. Rotate unit 180 degrees, reposition ruler, and trim. Block should now be 4½" wide. Repeat for remaining 2 sides so sashing square is 4½" square.

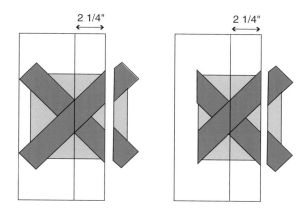

Sashing Square Trimming Diagrams

5. Repeat to make 35 sashing squares as shown in *Sashing Square Diagram*.

Sashing Square Diagram.

QUILT ASSEMBLY

1. Referring to *Quilt Assembly Diagram*, join 5 sashing squares and 4 sashing strips, positioning sashing squares so long cross bar always slants in the same direction, to make 1 sashing row. Repeat to make a total of 7 sashing rows.
2. To make 1 block row, choose 2 blocks with large bird facing right and 2 with large bird facing left. Join 4 blocks and 5 sashing strips. Make 6 block rows, alternating directions that birds face in each row and from row to row.
3. Join the sashing rows and the block rows, alternating types.

FINISHING

1. Mark quilting designs as desired. The quilt shown has a cable design in light areas of sashing strip units. Bird blocks are outline quilted around bird motifs with random meander quilting in background areas.

2. Divide backing fabric into 2 (1¾-yard) pieces. Split one piece in half lengthwise. Join half panels to sides of wide piece. Seams on quilt backing will run parallel to top and bottom quilt edges.

3. Layer quilt back, batting, and quilt top; baste.

4. Quilt as desired.

GARDEN MAZE SETTINGS

Garden maze is a setting you can use for virtually any quilt block or to feature an exciting printed fabric in a special way. For her Partridge Garden Maze quilt, Liz "fussy cut" motifs from a large scale print. When choosing a fabric to use in this manner, look for large, isolated print motifs.

The Garden Maze set of the Flower Pot quilt on page 70 creates the illusion of a trellis for the appliqué floral blocks. Garden maze is also an excellent way to feature pillow panels or "cheater patchwork" blocks.

To adapt this setting for your own blocks, simply adjust the length of the sashing strips to match your block size. As long as you use the same sashing width, the corner sashing squares will work.

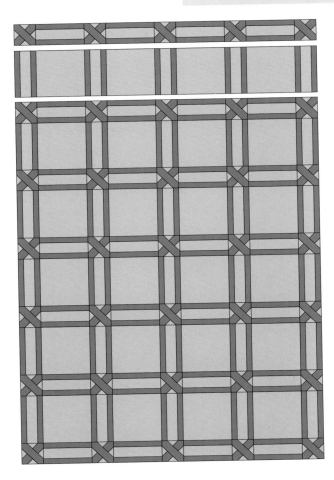

Quilt Assembly Diagram

ABOUT TV

We've been teaching quilting techniques on public television for several years now—through five series of our popular *Sew Many Quilts* program, and now with our new series called *Quilting with Fons & Porter*.

Filming a 13-episode series requires lots of work prior to the actual taping. We brainstorm to generate 13 interesting topics or projects, plan the sequences we will demonstrate, do lots of extra sewing to create "parts" of projects to work with on the air, organize our wardrobe (13 outfits each!), and then get all our equipment, supplies, and wardrobe to the studio.

At the studio, we work with a producer, director, assistant director, cameramen (and women), sound and lighting technicians, and our own assistant. The resulting series is the result of everyone's hard work, and we find it very satisfying. We generally tape all 13 episodes in about five days, filming as many as four episodes in one day! We tape all the "tip" sequences on the last day of the shoot.

Post production involves editing and closed-captioning and working with the satellite service that uplinks the shows. Also involved is providing information about the series to public television stations and to you, our viewers.

Quilting with Fons & Porter is a co-production with Iowa Public Television, our first series that is a joint effort with a public television affiliate.

The series began nationwide uplink January 1, 2000, to all public television stations. If the shows are not airing in your area, contact your local public television station and request them. Locate your station by visiting our internet website (www.fonsandporter.com) and following the links to TV. The instructions will ask you to enter your zip code to find your station. You can view your local schedule and also learn whom to call in the programming department.

Many viewers say our "tip" segment is their favorite part of the show. We enjoy receiving great quilting tips from viewers and sharing them on the show. If you have a tip you'd like to share, send it to:

Quilt Tips
Fons & Porter
P.O. Box 171
Winterset, IA 50273

If we use one of your tips on one of our shows, we'll send you our Perfect Binding Card, a laminated instruction sheet that tells you everything you need to know to make and add perfect binding to your quilts.

We love making quilts, and we enjoy teaching quilting skills to others, whether on television, through our books, on in person.

CREDITS

Co-Producers
Fons and Porter, L.C.
Iowa Public Television

Hosts
Marianne Fons and Liz Porter

Executive Producer
Duane Huey

Producers/Directors
Duane Huey
Andrea Coyle

Production Assistant
Shoney Jones

Special Guest
Marilyn Badger, Consultant
American Professional
Quilting Systems

Technical Directors
Carol Knight
Neal Kyer

Audio
Russell Wall
Jim Leasure

Video
Rod Turner
Karen Schweitzer

Camera Operators
Lyn Loheed
Amy Dougherty
Grant Hamilton
Aaron Finley

Scenic
Robert Sunderman

Electronic Graphics
Jeff Horn
Susan Peterson

Animation
Applied Art & Technology

Quilt Photographs
Sharon Risedorph

Author Photograph
Oxmoor House

Book Design
Lindsy Shelton
Chelle Farrand
C. Farrand Studios

Special Thanks To
Benartex, Inc.
Hewlett Packard
South Sea Imports
Displayaway Quilt Hangers
Jasmine Heirlooms

Fons & Porter Office
Ilene Kagarice, Office Manager
Katherine Herrick
Carol Selsor
Evalee Waltz
J.T. Ankeny

Quilts & Pre-Production
Assistance
Kelly Ashton
Kaye England
Marty Freed
Walda Gustafson
Katherine Herrick
Shoney Jones
Nancy Kirk, The Kirk Collection
Rozan Meacham
Carol Selsor
Evalee Waltz
Rhonda Richards
Ada Troyer
Katie Troyer
Vera Troyer
Amy Stewart Windsor
Lynn Witzenburg
Pat Yamin, Come Quilt With Me
Mary Yoder
Esther Zelinski

MAJOR FUNDING PROVIDED BY:

ADDITIONAL FUNDING PROVIDED BY:

Crafter's choice

BENARTEX
INCORPORATED

Friends
Iowa Public
Television

Omnigrid® Inc.

TV Program Notes

101 – Patchwork Alphabets
Fons and Porter teach you how to quick cut and piece your ABCs in fabric.

102 – Signature Quilts
Learn how to organize a signature quilt to commemorate an important family occasion.

103 – Early American Fabrics and Quilts
What fabrics did early American quilters use? Marianne and Liz share authentic examples and current reproductions.

104 – Plantation Star
Learn easy techniques to piece an unusual block based on square-in-a-square units.

105 – Southern Comfort
Liz and Marianne make cutting and combining triangles and squares easy to understand.

106 – Millennium Machine Quilting
Machine quilting expert Marilyn Badger is Liz and Marianne's guest demonstrator.

107 – Album Cross
Marianne and Liz demonstrate quick techniques for making a pattern that was popular with quilters during the Civil War.

108 – Color Copier Quilts
Fons & Porter show how to use ink jet color photocopying technology to create unique memory quilts.

109 – The Yo-Yo Show
Fabric circle yo-yos were made by the thousands in the 1930s. Fons and Porter share projects that require only a few, or many.

110 – Pansy Baby Quilt
Liz and Marianne combine innovative appliqué techniques and 1930s-style fabrics to create a charming crib-sized quilt.

111 – Prosperity Wheel
Marianne and Liz take the mystery out of machine piecing gentle curves for an unusual block inspired by an antique quilt.

112 – Flower Pot Appliqué
Learn some special short cuts to prepare flowers, stems, leaves, and flower pots for straight-stitch appliqué.

113 – Garden Maze Sets
This special setting is a great vehicle for showcasing unique fabrics. Liz and Marianne's special quick techniques make this once challenging quilt layout simple.